If Only My Patients Could Speak —

English, That Is!

To, Mary & Yvonne.

Dean E. Ewing, DVM

Shirley Herd

by Dean E. Ewing, DVM
and Shirley Herd

Foreword by Philip K. Ensley, DVM

S. Deal & Associates
Manitou Springs, Colorado

First printing 1995

Library of Congress Cataloging-in-Publication Data

Ewing, Dean E. (Dean Edgar), 1932-
    If only my patients could speak--English, that is! / by Dean E.
Ewing and Shirley Herd ; foreword by Philip K. Ensley.
        p.   cm.
    ISBN 0-930006-04-6
    1. Ewing, Dean E. (Dean Edgar), 1932-   . 2. Veterinarians-
-California--San Diego--Biography. 3. Pets--California--San Diego-
-Aneccdotes. 4. Animals--Anecdotes. I. Herd, Shirley, 1935-   .
II. Title.
SF613.E95A3 1995
636.089'092--dc20
    [B]   95-4553
                                                                    CIP

Printed in the United States of America

FOREWORD

Every veterinarian enjoys fond memories of working with animals and often their owners. In the long run these memories serve as the true compensation for the career chosen.

What Dean Ewing has experienced and now shares with us are a few of those countless memories. The stories he gives us are delivered with profound descriptions and with subtle punches.

Knowing Dean as I have over the years, I have always looked forward to his phone calls. He would call me at the Zoo or Wild Animal Park and have a question about some unfamiliar furry or feathered pet, hoping I could be of help. He always sounded so serious, trying to get to the bottom of any number of unique ailments. Dean always tried his hardest and always did his best. This comes through in his book and undoubtedly if his patients could speak they would tell you the same.

In a favorite story Dean tells of a peacock named "Buzzy." It is a favorite because I too am part of the story; and, it's a story that I often tell.

After reading this book you will have your favorite story and even if you were not there, you will feel as though you were.

Philip K. Ensley, DVM
Diplomat, ACZM

Diplomat, American College of Zoological Medicine
Associate Veterinarian Zoological Society of San Diego
American Veterinary Medical Association
American Association of Zoo Veterinarians
Association of Avian Veterinarians
Wildlife Disease Association
American Association of Zoological Parks and Aquariums
San Diego County Veterinary Medical Association
American Association of Zoo Keepers
Vulture Study Group

DEDICATION

I wish to acknowledge my appreciation to my wife, Shirley Herd (Ewing), for her help, encouragement and patience as we struggled to bring this book to fruition. Her unique literary ability, previous success as a writer and her broad knowledge make this effort a most enjoyable reading experience. To her, I dedicate this book.

PREFACE

As a youth in Indiana, I split my time between my grandfather's farm and my home in the city and as far back as I can remember, I loved animals. Because this adoration continued through high school, I decided to purse a career dedicated to animals and entered the field of veterinary medicine. I graduated from Michigan State University in 1956 with a Doctor of Veterinary Medicine degree and soon entered the US Air Force as an officer in the Veterinary Corps.

I never imagined when I entered the military how varied my experiences would be or how far afield from animals some of my duties would take me. I obtained a Masters degree in Radiation Biology and served as Chief of Bioastronautics where I was responsible for the radiobiological support of such space programs as Gemini, Apollo and Skylab. I served as the chief medical officer in the Defense Civil Preparedness Agency and then finally had an opportunity to work full-time with animals. I spent the last two years of my twenty-two year military career as Chief of the Veterinary Support Group, Naval Ocean Systems Center, in San Diego where I was responsible for the health and medical care of the US Navy's marine mammals.

Even though I did not work directly with animals for many years, I never lost my interest or love for them. I attended veterinary seminars, worked with local associations and read current journals and literature to keep abreast of new medicines and procedures. When I retired from the Air Force, I followed the most logical avenue for a veterinarian: I opened a small animal practice in San Diego, specializing in avians.

When I spoke or presented papers to groups of medical professionals, I often pointed out a major difference between a physician and a veterinarian. A physician has a limited practice, one species, while a veterinarian treats many species. In addition, a physician usually has the helpful input of the patient telling him what or where he or she hurts. However, because an animal cannot speak — English, that is — a veterinarian must rely heavily on the signs and symptoms that the animal presents, history obtained from the owner and a large dose of intuition before making a diagnosis.

Although the names of the animals and people used in this book may have been changed, the stories are true. I am pleased to share some of these unusual, informative or heart-warming episodes with you. Perhaps through this sharing, you will have a better understanding of your animal as well as the frequently puzzling position of a veterinarian.

I hope you will enjoy reading my stories as much as I have had in experiencing them. Happy reading.

Dean E. Ewing DVM

Dean E. Ewing, DVM

TABLE OF CONTENTS

Pyrenees • Spike, pit bulldog • Chow-Chow, chow •
Numerous Great Danes

Chapter 11
LOVE THEM ALL   199

Cat ladies • Cats, cats and more cats • Many animals
including Doc, the Mollucan cockatoo • Trying to breed dogs

MILITARY ASSIGNMENTS

Chapter 12
MARINE MAMMALS   219

Sea lions, seals and dolphins • Ivan the Terrible, Pacific
dolphin • Pandora, Atlantic bottlenosed dolphin • Liberty,
California sea lion • A trio of sea lions • Treating sea lions •
A dolphin and the SEAL team • Harbor seals • Beluga whales
• Alaskan fur seal

Chapter 13
ISLAND ADVENTURES   235

San Miguel Island: sea lions, elephant seals, island fox and
other wildlife • Oahu, Hawaii: training sessions with Rex, the
dolphin

Chapter 14
TREKKING THROUGH THAILAND   249

Stories and experiences during a one-year tour in Thailand •
Cross-bred beef and dairy cattle • Rice birds, silk worms and
beetles • Thai cavalry • Treating pets • Henry, monitor lizard •
Hornbill • Song birds • Lizards • Snakes, pickled and alive •
Centipede • Vaccinating dogs for rabies • Doctor Boonsong
and native birds • Hawk-eagle • Sentry dogs • Water buffalo

San Diego,

California

1

Curious Cases

Cloak-and-dagger escapades are not limited to spies or undercover agents but sometimes can involve pet owners and their pets. Basic facts such as the owner's name, phone number or address remain unsolved mysteries when the pet or pets requiring veterinary treatment are illegal to own. Undoubtedly, the owners believe that the veterinarian will tell the appropriate agency and the animals will be confiscated. This must have been the reasoning of the woman who phoned me at my office.

"I understand you have experience treating marine mammals," she said.

"Yes, I do. I've been in charge of the health and well being of the mammals for the Navy. Why? Do you know where there's an animal in need of treatment?" I asked, thinking that she had perhaps discovered an ailing sea lion or seal on the beach.

"As a matter of fact, there are two — two Malaysian otters. They don't seem to be eating as much as they usually do and appear to be losing weight."

Obviously these animals were not stranded on a local beach because they are native to Malaysia, a country located between Thailand and Singapore in southeast Asia, so they must be in one of the city's animal parks. "Are you calling from Sea World or the zoo?"

"No, neither." There was a silence. "No," she said again. "They are mine."

I caught my breath and fell silent for a moment. She had definitely surprised me with that answer! Numerous questions flitted instantly through my mind — where was she keeping the otters that required water to swim in, what was she feeding them, were they well cared for?

"I'm sure you know that they are not legal pets in San Diego." I stopped, waiting for her reply but only heard her sigh. "However," I continued, "putting that aside, what can I do to help them and, first, what is your name?"

"I don't want to tell you my name," she answered quickly. "Just call me Mary and my otters are Pat and Mike and — " Now her words flowed as rapidly as a tumbling waterfall as she explained the ailing otters symptoms. From her description of their condition, I needed to examine them.

"I really must see them, to check them and do some basic testing. I can come out tomorrow." I grabbed my pen. "What's your address?"

"No," she replied quite firmly and without a hesitation. "It would be better if I brought Pat and Mike to you."

"Well," I rubbed the stubble on my chin while I wondered which facility might allow me to examine two illegal pets. "I need to make a couple of phone calls to find a place and set up a time. I'll call you back when I have it arranged." Again I poised my pen above the notepaper. "What's your phone number?"

Silence. Then she stammered, "I have to — have to run some errands so it would be better if I called you back. Do you think you'll know something in about two hours?"

"Yes. Call back then."

As I hung up the receiver, I thought how successfully she had avoided giving me any information about her. Definitely, she was doing her best to keep the whereabouts of her pets a secret.

She called back and said she would meet me but actually, I was surprised when she arrived on time the next afternoon at the designated local veterinary clinic. Because of her evasive attitude, I knew she did not think she could trust me to keep the existence of her pets a secret but, obviously her concern over their health had overcome her fear of discovery.

We walked out to her station wagon where Pat and Mike barked out a greeting as they actively squirmed and rolled about in their individual cages. She opened the hatchback door and I could see that each animal was a dark slate color with healthy-looking sleek fur — a visual sign that their diet might be appropriate. Each mammal weighed, I guessed, about thirty pounds and was at least twice as big as a house cat.

"Let me give you a hand carrying them," Mary offered. "They're awkward to handle in cages."

"Thanks." We each lifted a side of the cage and transported the otters one at a time into the examining room. I wondered who had helped her lift them into the wagon. Although she was not a fragile-looking woman, on the other hand, she definitely did not pump iron. Maybe there was a "Mister X" who helped her. And perhaps this same man had sent Pat and Mike from southeast Asia to the States because he was or still is in government service and had been stationed over there. Chances are I would never know how these otters got to San Diego because I felt sure if I asked, she would respond with another noncommittal answer.

I observed them in the cages, looking for anything unusual. Satisfied that their appearance looked normal, I asked, "Will you please move Mike to the examining table for me?" She nodded, opened the cage and lifted the squirming mass to the table, keeping a firm grip on him.

I talked soothingly to Mike and reached out to palpate him with as much caution as I would any wild, native otter with threatening sharp teeth. Although these mammals were pets and used to being around people, I did not know how either of them would react to a stranger, particularly one who wanted to poke, probe and eventually prick them.

Both otters barked and wiggled continually trying to get away from Mary and me during the entire checkup and the taking of blood and fecal samples but the two were manageable. The only thing I discovered from the hands-on exam when I listened with the stethoscope was an unusual resonance from the lungs.

"Overall, they both seem in good health except for a possible respiratory infection. Before I suggest any kind of treatment, I want to get the tests results back to find out if they have any other problems that aren't evident. I should know by tomorrow. I'll call you with the results if you like." I grinned, knowing her well enough by now that she would not give me her phone number.

She smiled at me warmly but with eyes that echoed distrust. "No, thanks. I'll call you. Tomorrow afternoon?"

"That'll be fine. Sometime after two."

Together, we carted the caged animals back to her car, she got in and nodded a farewell. I waved back to the mysterious "Madame X" and watched as she made a speedy exit — probably faster than she usually drove so that I could not easily read her license plate numbers.

The test results showed that the otters were in relatively good health with the exception of a minor decrease in red blood cells and an increase in white blood cells that indicated a slight case of anemia and a possible bacterial infection. With this data and my findings during the physical exam, I suspected an early respiratory disease. Although normals were not available for this species of otter, by comparing Pat's and Mike's results with those of other aquatic animals and calling friends at the zoo for their input, I came up with a proper antibiotic dosage by the time Mary phoned.

"On the basis of the tests and exams I feel we definitely are dealing with a respiratory infection that requires medication. In addition, I suggest you give them a daily vitamin and mineral supplement to correct the anemia. I can meet you at four at the clinic with the medicines or — I can deliver them." No harm in trying one more time.

"Thanks anyway," she replied. "I need to run some errands in that part of town so I'll meet you."

Mary arrived promptly. I handed her the medications, discussed the treatment and how to get the antibiotics and vitamins and minerals easily into the otters by putting them inside their favorite fish.

"Naturally, I'm curious about where you keep Pat and Mike."

She smiled. "They have wonderful accommodations. A swimming pool of their own, a private back yard with a high fence covered by shrubs and vines so they can't get out — and so people can't see in."

"It sounds wonderful. Could I come out and see it and check them over again?" I had hoped that by now she had enough confidence in me to let me examine the otters in their own environment.

"Sorry, Doctor, that's not possible."

"Then, you must call me in two days and let me know how they're responding to the medication."

"I will." She turned and walked away, undoubtedly to her car that this time was parked out of sight from the clinic.

As promised, she called to say they were doing well and, at my request, said she would call me back in ten days with an additional report. True to her word, she phoned again to say both otters were fine. That was the last time I ever heard from the mysterious Mary.

A case such as this does not happen too often but when it does, there are distinct advantages for the veterinarian who, like other small business owners, has problems with receivables. Because the owner does not wish to be located, no information-giving checks with a name and address are offered that could be returned stamped "insufficient funds" and no installment payment plans are needed whose deadlines are frequently not met. All fees by owners wishing to remain anonymous are handled immediately and with cash.

What started out as a simple act to amuse the bird ended up as a most unique, time-consuming "surgery" that required no incising of the epidermis but quite the opposite — trying not to cut it.

Birds are attracted to bright, shiny objects and the owner's massive ring with sparkling stone was eye-catching to the African gray parrot. Bob removed his one-half-inch wide ring and, with some pushing, forcing and maneuvering, slid it over the bird's foot. Popeye admired it, tried to bite and play with it for a while and then became bored with it. The owner seeing the bird was disinterested tried to remove it and could not because, by now, Popeye had a swollen leg.

The owner waited twenty-four hours before calling me and by the time I arrived, the only way to remove the ring was to cut it off — as soon as possible — before the circulation to the foot was completely interrupted and amputation necessary. I placed the attractive two-toned gray bird with red tail feathers in a carrying cage and took him to the clinic where I had not only the necessary tools but the required assistants. One person would have to hold the twelve-inch long bird in the towel while the other one held the leg steady and dripped water on the area to keep it cool because I would be cutting with a Dremel saw which causes heat through friction.

Before I could even start to cut, however, I needed to score the area to prevent the blade from slipping. With a pair of wire cutters, I notched the ring then began to saw most carefully. Even with my assistant dripping water continuously, I could only work about a minute at a time because the metal would get uncomfortably hot. The intermittent cutting and waiting continued until finally, I had sawed the ring all the way through.

"Phew," I breathed a sigh of success, relieved that this tedious job was finished. "I'm glad that's over. Now, let's pry it apart."

Such an easy statement to say but an impossible act to perform! We tried and tried again to bend the ring open far enough to slip the leg out but it was still too solid a mass to bend.

"I guess I spoke too soon. I'm going to have to make another cut."

All heads bent over the bird, I made another notch-cut about one-quarter inch from the first and the process began again. Two hours from the time we started, the metal had weakened enough to pull the ring apart and remove it. Popeye was fine, no cuts or harm had occurred but as to the condition of the ring — I doubt if the owner would be wearing it soon, if ever.

Monroe was a small five- to six-weeks-old black and white kitten with vivid yellow eyes whose owner,

Stacy, brought him into the clinic for a routine checkup and vaccinations. I never guessed during that first visit that Monroe would develop a fat file folder filled with mysterious or unusual reactions, illnesses or physical abnormalities.

After his exam and vaccinations, I returned to Stacy, sitting in the waiting room. "Monroe seems to be quite a healthy kitten — I could find nothing wrong." I scratched his silky hair behind the ear and then handed him to her.

"Thanks, Doctor," Stacy said as she put him in his carrying cage. "That's good news. When should I bring him in again?"

"In two or three weeks for a second shot in this series, then three or four weeks after that for the last of the series. When he's four months old, bring him in for a rabies vaccination and when he's six months old, for neutering."

"Okay. See you later." She smiled and left, Monroe mewing as she walked out the door.

About four days later, Stacy called. "You know the vaccinations you gave Monroe?"

"Yes. Is something wrong?"

"I can feel a lump on the side of his neck."

In most cats, the tiny lump that can develop usually goes away in two or three days. Apparently Monroe was having a mild reaction to the shot. "Hmm," I said, "I think it will go away in a few more days but let me know if it does not."

Stacy called back three days later to say it had taken a week but the lump had disappeared, however, now the kitten had another problem. "I don't know what's wrong but he has a swollen lower lip. I think you better look at him. Can I bring him in tomorrow?"

The oral exam the next day showed a most unique condition. Cats have a small pocket in the lower lip that the canine teeth fit into. Monroe's baby canine teeth, however, were not aligned properly and did not go into these pockets. The two teeth were going over the slots and rubbing, irritating the lip tissue which was causing his swollen mouth.

"This is most unusual and I think you should see Doctor Mulligan, a veterinary dental specialist, for a more complete evaluation."

Stacy glanced down at the floor, a worried frown crisscrossing her forehead. "I'm afraid I don't have a great deal of money. Naturally, I love my little kitten and want the best for him so — I guess — " I could tell by her thoughtful pause she was mentally weighing her income versus possible medical expenses. She sighed. "What's Doctor Mulligan's phone number?"

I gave her the number and assured her that most veterinarians are willing to work with clients regarding payment. "Please let me know what he recommends."

I did not have to wait for Stacy's call because Doctor Mulligan called me shortly after examining Monroe. He said he had never seen anything like this before nor could he find any information regarding a similar case in any of his medical journals or books. He recommended removing the canine teeth now because if we waited the four or five months for the teeth to fall out by themselves, too much trauma would have occurred to the lower lip. He hoped that by extracting the baby teeth, when the adult teeth came in, they would be in alignment with the pockets. I agreed and Monroe had oral surgery.

Only a few weeks passed when Stacy called me again. "His surgery went well and the swelling in his lower lip is gone but now he has another problem. Fleas."

San Diego is known as a flea capital and I have often thought that if the skin-related dermatitis and other problems that develop from flea bites did not exist, half the veterinarians in town would be out of business. "Fleas are definitely a problem here and most pets in town have varying degrees of skin irritation but, what is happening to Monroe?"

"I've tried various brands of flea collars and sprays from pet stores and supermarkets but he has a severe reaction to all of them. He salivates, staggers when he walks and, in general, is uncoordinated. What should I do?"

I have alerted people to the dangers of over-the-counter flea products for cats because cats tend to have a high probability of a reaction that sometimes can even be life-threatening. I found that the reaction may not be caused by the insecticide but by the other chemical agents used with the insecticide. On the other hand, flea products prescribed by a veterinarian do not usually cause a reaction to most cats.

I thought about giving him an oral flea control pill that contained a small dose of insect poison so that when the flea bites the animal, the parasite dies. I decided just as rapidly that although a cat two months old probably could safely take the drug, because of Monroe's past history of reactions to medications, it possibly could cause unpre-dictable side effects.

"Well," I hesitated, "I can formulate a mild solution of a flea dip that you can apply directly to the troubled areas and use sparingly. Perhaps, he can tolerate a small amount of it as opposed to a full body application. If he doesn't have a reaction, I'll gradually increase the strength of the mixture. In addition, buy a flea comb and comb him daily as I instructed you during your last visit."

The combination of the two remedies controlled the flea problem but soon Stacy brought Monroe in again because he had another ailment: a severe case of diarrhea. I ran routine tests and discovered he had excessive amounts of foreign matter such as lint in his feces. Apparently, when she was not home, he would get bored and lick the carpet, bedspread or other fabrics ingesting the substances. I suggested that Stacy confine him in an area where he did not have access to these materials, possibly the bathroom, and hoped that he would outgrow this vice.

Monroe, now only four months old, was back to see me again and was fast becoming one of my most frequently seen patients. Stacy brought him in because he was running a temperature of 104 degrees. My first thought was that he must have an infection so I ran routine tests — that showed only a slightly elevated white blood cell count, not a reason for the temperature. I kept him in the clinic for observation for two days but discovered nothing so sent him home with antibiotics. Since Monroe was such a problem cat, I was very concerned about his condition so I instructed the owner to take his temperature and call me daily.

Stacy called me each of the next three days to say Monroe was still not feeling well and continued to run a fever. Because all the tests showed nothing wrong with him, the only probable cause left was FUO — Fevers of Unknown Origin. These fevers are not uncommon in cats and generally I treat two or three cases of FUO a year. Although there is a complete chapter in one of my medical texts about FUO, little is known about why these mysterious fevers appear then eventually disappear when the cat gets older. Usually when dealing with such cases, I administer an injection of medicine that causes the body temperature to drop but because of Monroe's background of unusual reactions to medication, I was not sure how it would effect him. I did not want to cure one problem and create another yet there was little else to do so I decided I had to try it.

Stacy brought Monroe in every three days for a shot for two weeks. During that time, she gave me a daily condition report concerning how Monroe was responding and, as mysteriously as the fever appeared, in two weeks, it went away.

Then at five months, Monroe developed eosinophilic granuloma, a skin disease which occurs in several areas of the body but is most often seen on the face, lips and neck. It, too, is a condition of unknown origin but is possibly related to a hormone and/or immune system defect. This disease is fairly common in younger cats who generally tend to outgrow it in a few months to a year; however, when it develops in older cats, it is most difficult to get rid of. Fortunately for Monroe, he was still young and should overcome it. I put him on steroids and topical medicines and, amazingly, he responded quite well with no side effects.

By this time, I had so many conversations with and visitations by Stacy — who originally erroneously thought she would not see me except for shots and neutering — that she and the cat almost seemed a part of my family. I wondered what unusual occurrence would happen next to Monroe. I did not have to wait long for the answer.

Stacy brought Monroe to me for his "routine" neutering. I should have known nothing would be routine for Monroe because as my surgical technician was preparing Monroe for surgery, she exclaimed, "Look at this, Doctor! I think he only has one testicle."

I quickly examined the area and she was right. How on earth could I have overlooked this during his numerous examinations? Although I was chagrined, I was not too surprised because I was dealing with Monroe, a cat with a track record for the unexpected.

"Prep him for abdominal surgery," I responded.

I had to try to locate the testicle because if not found Monroe would have a high probability of testicular cancer in later years. After the incision was made, I searched methodically and thoroughly but never could find it. Perhaps Monroe was born with only one testicle or it was so underdeveloped and small that I could not locate it or, if there, it was in a place where I could not find it. I sutured him then removed the visible testicle while hoping that the illusive one would not cause a problem for Monroe in the future.

All stories have a conclusion and Monroe's is a happy one. Like many children who seem to be sickly during infancy and childhood and then quite healthy in their teens and adulthood, his pattern was the same. In the chart equating feline to human years, a six-month-old cat equals a thirteen-year-old child. Monroe, who definitely had more than the average cat's "childhood" illnesses and problems, had finally outgrown them. At three and a half years old, the equivalent to a thirty-six-year-old human, Monroe was a healthy cat.

S am was indeed a pathetic sight. Although he was a white furred miniature poodle, he had an overall pinkish cast highlighted by numerous yellow crusty patches all over his body. He appeared to be suffering from a severe allergy that caused his skin to be red and inflamed. The crusty areas were formed by the weeping of the irritated epidermis as a result of the condition. A flea induced allergic skin problem generally is localized and appears on the back over the pelvis, down the tail and sometimes under the legs. However, in Sam's case, his entire body was effected.

I rubbed my hands gently over him and he flinched when I barely touched certain areas indicating that those spots were tender. I cautiously picked at one of the flaking areas and a patch of Sam's hair came out with the flakes!

"Seems Sam really has a skin problem. Has he been this way long?"

"About three months," Nita replied. "I've been to another veterinarian without success and I heard you have a high success rate dealing with dermatological problems. I simply don't know what to do, how to treat it or for that matter, what's wrong."

"It's possible he's just allergic to something or he's deficient in a vitamin or mineral. I need to run a few tests and I think we'll know more.

The fourteen-year-old Sam's test results showed no infections, a normal bacterial count and a negative viral test. In other words, I had no clue as to what was wrong. If he was allergic to something, it would have to be found by eliminating or adding certain foods or it was possible that environmental factors might even be the cause.

I called Nita and reported my findings — or lack of them — and suggested treating him with steroids, giving him medicated baths, hypoallergenic foods and making sure he had good nutrition. "In addition, I want to increase his vitamin C intake to help his immune system."

Two months went by and still there was no dramatic change. I suggested trying an immune system stimulant and other immune system support. At the same time, I inten-

sified the topical treatments to control the external symptoms as much as possible. The situation would fluctuate,
looking better for a short time and then regress. After
several weeks on this medication protocol, there was still
no dramatic improvement, let alone a cure. The medicated
shampoos and other topical medications seemed to make
him more comfortable although they did not get rid of the
dry patches or lessen his redness.

The months slowly grew into a year and still Sam
was not showing any marked improvement. What had I
overlooked or missed? His problem was not common or
discussed in any of my veterinary journals or books. So —
what had I read elsewhere?

I thoughtfully swiveled in my desk chair, trying to
come up with something when — a client's problem
popped into mind. She had mentioned to me the difficulty
she was having with a systemic yeast infection. Suppose
Sam has this? I had not read any studies about animals
having a systemic yeast infection, yet, all things are possible.

I called Nita and explained to her that I would like to
verify this possibility with a diagnostic test. She agreed and
brought Sam in.

The test was inconclusive but I felt I was on the right
track. "Nita, would you consider trying Sam on ketoconazole, a drug that is used to combat yeast infections in
humans. I must tell you, first, that it will be expensive."

"How expensive?" she asked.

"It will probably run about one hundred dollars a
month."

There was only a brief reflective silence and she answered, "Yes. At this point, I'm willing to do anything to help Sam."

Within two weeks after the beginning of this medication and the continuation of the shampoos, Sam showed improvement. I was elated and Nita ecstatic. "He still has a skin problem," she reported, "but he's so much better." Her words had a zesty bounce to them.

"It may take many months, even years, or there is the chance that he may never be totally cured. We'll just have to wait to see what happens."

"I understand," she replied. "I'm just so relieved that he is better. Thanks again, Doctor."

At the last checking, one year later, Sam was still getting periodic treatments of ketoconazole, had less than a normal amount of hair but with the use of a solid total health care program of nutrition, medicated baths and supportive topical treatments was doing quite well. As for my findings, I believe that systemic yeast infections may be more common among animals than most veterinarians suspect.

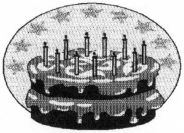

"Something terrible has happened to Sweet Pea!" Lila blurted out over the phone. "He's a chocolate-covered disaster. Not only did he eat an entire cake but he rolled in the crumbs and frosting. What should I do?"

I treat several cases a year of animals poisoned by insecticides and rat poisons and, although I am a chocaholic and find it hard to believe one could ever get too much of it, for a dog too much chocolate can be life-threatening. The toxic dose of chocolate for a dog ranges from 0.25 to 0.7 ounces of baking chocolate per pound of weight to 2.5 to 5.0 ounces of milk chocolate per pound of weight. The result of ingesting too much chocolate can be excitability, restlessness, tremors, seizures, coma and can even cause permanent heart damage. I needed to start treatment on Sweet Pea immediately.

"Bring him in as fast as you can. His life can depend on it."

Within fifteen minutes, Lila and her mischievous miniature black poodle entered the clinic. What a mess! Chocolate frosting clung to him like moss to a tree. Although he was trembling and excited, according to Lila, he had not had any seizures yet.

My assistant wrapped him in a towel and quickly took him to the grooming area for a bath.

"Will he be all right?" she asked, wiping chocolate from her hands and blouse with a tissue.

"I'll begin treating him immediately and we'll know more tomorrow. Do I have your permission for an elec-trocardiogram to find out if there has been any heart damage and for a blood panel if necessary?"

"Yes. Absolutely."

"Fine. I'll call you as soon as I know anything."

I dashed from the room to check on Sweet Pea's cleanup procedure which would be followed by Toxaban®, a charcoal based substance that is forced into the intestinal tract to tie up and absorb the toxin. He would then need intravenous fluids and medication.

Later that day when his condition had been stabilized, I prepared him for the EKG. I did not need to own this sophisticated, costly piece of equipment because cardiovascular diagnostics can be done by telephone using specialists that were, for me, 3,000 miles away in New York City. I placed the four leads on Sweet Pea, dialed the telephone and transmitted the data. If needed, the results are available within the hour or, if not a critical case, the results are ready the next day and a hard copy of the tracing sent the next week so that it can be included in the animal's permanent records.

I called Lila as soon as I received Sweet Pea's readings. "Good news. His chocolate-eating binge caused no heart problems and he is almost back to normal."

"Phew," she exhaled a sigh of relief. "Thank heavens. I think I'll sleep better tonight than I did last night. When can he come home?"

"You should be able to pick him up later this afternoon."

"Great. And, you better believe that the next time I bake a chocolate cake, I'm not putting it on the table. It's going on top of the refrigerator, far, far away from my chocolate-loving dog."

Strange things can happen to animals when they are outside, even when the owners are present. Jan and George were out on their lighted patio about midnight watching their pet duck swim in its water-filled fiberglass pool when suddenly from out of the dark, a coastal fox, twice as big as a house cat, darted. Much to the horror of the surprised owners, the fox attacked the duck and dislocated one of the wings before they could scare it away. Thinking fast, they managed to put the wing back into place and although the duck had several lacerations that I treated the next day and it was sick for the next three days, it did recover.

Even stranger things can happen to animals that are allowed to roam outdoors unattended. An animal is exposed to the threats of being killed by an automobile, eating a toxic substance, getting in fights with other animals, being "adopted" by a well-meaning person who thinks the pet is a stray, to this bizarre story about Rambo, the gray tabby cat. Indeed, there are many good reasons to keep your beloved pet in the house.

I had seen Rambo, a two- to three-year-old neutered male, periodically for shots or checkups. He was a healthy cat whose owner, unfortunately, permitted him the freedom of the outdoor life even though I had warned Sue about the possible dangers involved with this lifestyle.

"Doctor Ewing, there's something not quite right with Rambo. I want you to look at him."

"What is it? Is he sick or hurt?"

"No, I don't think he's sick but he may be — I dunno. He's got something on his stomach — I'm not sure what. Can I bring him in and maybe you can explain it?"

"Of course," I answered, puzzled by her lack of symptoms and curious as to what might be wrong. "I'll see you about two this afternoon."

Sue and Rambo were waiting for me in the examining room when I returned from lunch. "Hello, Sue. What's the problem?"

"Well — I know your going to tell me "I told you so" for letting Rambo run loose but — he disappeared for about two weeks. I searched the neighborhood, put up posters, called Animal Control and all the shelters and could not find him. I had given up hope when yesterday he came home. I picked him up and started petting him when I felt something funny on his stomach. Take a look."

I rolled Rambo over and examined his stomach. There was a recently made incision line and the unusual items that Sue felt were the closing sutures.

I had to chuckle because the veterinarian who performed this surgery must have been surprised and embarrassed when he or she opened up the cat.

"What's so funny?" she asked.

"Well, it seems as though this is a case of mistaken identity. Your cat has not only been neutered but now he's been spayed — at least an attempted spaying."

Sue looked puzzled. "What?"

"Doubtlessly, the person who found Rambo must have thought he was a she because the cat had no testicles and took it to a veterinarian for spaying. The doctor, also noting the absence of the obvious and taking the person's word that this was a female, operated only to discover the true sex of the cat. More than likely, Rambo was sutured, by a red-faced veterinarian who sheepishly returned him to whomever brought him in."

"Good heavens! Is he all right?"

"Yes. The incision is healing fine. Now," I looked at her sternly over the rim of my glasses, "let's talk about letting him roam outside."

As a veterinarian specializing in avians, I had treated unique cases but for two birds, a white cockatiel and a white cockatoo, to have the same accident occur within a week of one another is as unusual as the incidents. The white cockatoo or Moluccan was about eighteen-inches long with a white crest and is native to Indonesia. The cockatiel was only about ten-inches long, had a yellow crest, rosy-orange cheek patches and is from Australia.

Both birds were brought in because the owners discovered a bleeding area above the anus and below the tail feathers. Each bird had fallen off a perch and during the fall had caught its long tail feathers on some object that pushed the feathers abruptly up and tore the skin. Both required stitches, were treated for infection systemically and topically and both recovered. After all these years treating birds, I still have not seen other such cases.

Birds in the wild have numerous mishaps and many hazards to contend with and most of them are caused by man or man-made products. I have treated many pelicans, not a well-liked bird by fishermen, that had been purposely shot or had hooks lodged in their bills or fishing line wrapped around their bills, legs, wings or toes. Pelicans respond well to treatment if they are well enough to eat but are hard to handle and difficult to treat. A pelican

can bite hard enough to leave a nasty bruise or even a bleeding wound so its bill must be taped shut in order to examine or treat it. However, great care must be taken not to tape the bill too tightly because a pelican breathes through its mouth.

Along with pigeons and doves, gulls are fairly hardy birds although, judging by the predicaments gulls get into, they are not too bright. I have treated them for gunshot wounds, removed fishing lines, fish hooks and strangling six-pack holders from around their necks and numerous objects wrapped around their toes.

Herons, egrets, cranes and sand pipers were brought to me because of the same type of accidents plus they were sometimes hit by a car, had been attacked by a predator or had ingested bottle caps, hooks or plastic objects. A few had flown into wires and needed everything from amputated wings or legs to simple general care. I was able to release about fifty percent of the wild birds I treated. For critical cases, organizations in my area such as Project Wildlife, the Wildlife Center and Wildlife Rescue had dollars and volunteers to help and care for them.

Treating accidents is an expected part of a veterinarian's profession, however, the care or treatment of a hurt animal or bird because of man's thoughtless actions is always unpleasant to deal with. Each of us can do something to prevent needless injuries to our wildlife by being more conscientious and cautious when discarding unwanted items.

Strange Bedfellows

Spring brings the budding of trees, the greening of dormant plants and the birth of many animals — sadly, because many of them are unwanted by their owners. Spaying or neutering of family pets would prevent this birthing explosion that, in turn, means finding homes or giving them to shelters or, in some cases, the heartless abandonment of pets that leaves them to fend for themselves. Like other veterinarians, I have treated or nursed to health many unclaimed, unwanted or near-death animals without charge simply because I could not bear to see them suffer for lack of proper care.

Frequently, the necessary treatment was done more easily in my home than a clinic so a variety of animals became my roommates until I could find homes for them or I became so attached to their delightful personalities that I kept them. It was not unusual to have cats, exotic birds, hamsters, reptiles and other strays in separate cages but all sharing the same general quarters.

In such a family environment, instinctive enemies become tolerant of one another and observing their interactions quite rewarding and sometimes hard to believe. One relationship so unique developed between two of my pets — Comet, a cat, and Keo, a budgie — that when a local television station heard about it, they became stars of the five o'clock news!

Comet was one of those all too numerous abandoned animals that came to live with me. A passerby heard weak mews coming from a garbage can, looked into the metal coffin and found a scrawny, weak seven- to ten-day-old kitten so covered with fleas and flea bites she was on the verge of needing a blood transfusion. The concerned woman immediately took her to the nearest qualified help, a wildlife center in Poway, for care and treatment. At that time, I was volunteering my services to the center and saw the pathetic kitten. She would require a great deal of care and no one there had the time to give it to her because of the demands of the other animals, so I decided to keep her.

Even in her pitiful state, she was a beautifully marked female kitten with a midnight black coat, four white-gloved paws, a white-vested chest and belly and a distinctive white streaking mark on her forehead that re-sembled a shooting star, a comet. I took her home, flea-bathed her and fed her kitten milk replacement about every four hours from a nursing bottle until she was strong and old enough to eat on her own. With the fleas under control and a wholesome diet, she soon lived up to her name in another respect: She zipped and darted from one mischie-vous act to another with the speed of a fast-moving comet.

Comet, like all kittens, was playful but in addition to the usual kitten antics, she enjoyed doing tricks. I easily trained her to shake paws, sit, walk on a leash and retrieve small thrown objects. She could even jump through a hoop made from a pulled-open coat hanger. By tempting her on one side of the loop with a piece of cheese or her favorite toy, a crinkled piece of cellophane, she would jump through it as skillfully as any trained lion in the circus.

She also was a "thinking" cat which she proved to me quite readily. She was a house cat who was only let outside when I went out and when she had on her leash. Because I always had yard chores to do, I devised a way to give her freedom to move about yet keep her under control. I took a board, put a hook in it and attached her leash to it which gave her about a five-foot radius in which to roam. For several months she accepted the tethered existence although not without a few meowing complaints about being tied. Then, one day I started outside with her leash in hand, calling her to come. She walked several steps with me, looked out longingly, then at her leash and turned back as if to say, "If I can't go out without being tied up, I won't go out at all." She never again wanted to go outside if the leash and board were necessary. Perhaps it was this reasoning, thinking ability that made the forthcoming relationship possible.

A few months after adopting Comet, I took home a seven-inch long female budgie, a type of parakeet, that had been diagnosed by the County Veterinarian as needing care and medication, to join the family group of cat, parrot, hamster and cockatiel. I named her Keo, Thai for green, after her brilliantly-colored feathers. Soon, with care, medicine and nourishing food, she noisily hopped around the cage, swung on her trapeze and was a playful, cheerful feathered companion that was easily finger-trained.

Life at home was a miniature zoo with notable squawks, chirps and the dashing about of a frisky cat all of which began every night after work with the sound of the front door key in the lock and my calling out their names. I looked forward to this six-day-a-week overture of sounds as a pleasant welcome home.

One night, however, I opened the door, called out, "Keo. Comet," and listened for the familiar bird sounds or a furry rush of response. Only a stillness, an ominous, foreboding silence filled the house.

I walked the few steps to the family room and stared with disbelief and horror at the empty wrought iron bird cage. The door was open, Keo gone — and where was Comet? A lump formed instantly in my throat and my pulse quickened. A bird and a cat left on the loose, left to nature's way for a few minutes or maybe even an entire workday! Quickly I scanned the cage and adjacent area looking for the inevitable — feathers, tufts of fur, blood or any signs of a skirmish. Nothing.

Perhaps Keo was quick or clever enough to escape Comet's playful leaps and managed somehow to climb to safety. She certainly could not fly with clipped wings. I glanced to the top of the couch, the cupboard, the adjacent kitchen counter and appliance top. No bird or signs of one and no telltale scratching of a pursuing cat.

I started down the hallway checking each room while a mental picture of my two six-month-old pets in a grisly fight flooded my thoughts. There was no doubt in my mind who the victor would be: The odds against a one-ounce bird surviving the sharp claws of a bounding, twelve-pound kitten would be about as good as pitting Pee Wee Herman against George Foreman.

The thought of losing either of them was devastating. Although as a veterinarian I have learned that no matter what surgical procedure I do or medication I prescribe, I cannot always save every pet, however, the death of any animal under my care is never easy to accept. In this instance, the forthcoming unpleasant scene I felt certain I would find was completely unnecessary. The whole pending tragedy had to be my fault because how else could the cage door be open unless I accidentally had left it that way?

I reached the turn in the corridor to the master bedroom, the only remaining area. I pictured it spotted with blood and littered with feathers. Undoubtedly, Comet was contentedly sprawled and sleeping on her favorite pillow, her belly well-rounded by a hearty dinner, completely oblivious to the humanly distasteful act she had committed.

I hesitated, took a deep breath and muttered, "No use prolonging the inevitable." I strode into the room mustering up the strength required to cope with the circumstances.

Instead of what I had imagined, I saw, much to my extreme relief, two intact pets on the king-sized bed. Each noticed me with a quick glance and immediately returned to play. Keo was strutting around the bed, a place she had never been allowed, while Comet from a pouncing position would leap at her, carefully avoiding touching her, then draw back, hunch up and leap again. The two were playing a game.

I watched them for a few minutes, overwhelmed by the care and caution the cat had for the bird. Comet, whose favorite pastime was staring out the patio glass door at every bird that came near with chin quivering and body in an attack mode, now was playing harmlessly with her natural prey. Keo, a bird who had been introduced to her first cat only recently, was allowing a dreaded natural enemy to leap at her with no apparent concern.

I picked up the budgie, gave her a loving caress while running my fingers over her tiny body to be sure she had not been harmed and carried her back to the family room. Comet followed us, mewing and intertwining her body with each of my foot steps.

"You were a good kitty, Comet," I said affectionately, "just playing with Keo and not hurting her. But, let's not press our luck any more today."

I put Keo on her perch, made sure the door was closed and bent down to rub Comet on her favorite under-the-chin spot. "You must be hungry — especially after being tempted for who knows how long by a delicious feathered dinner." When I fixed her supper that night, I scooped out a bit more cat food than she usually received and watched her as she hungrily wolfed it, not unprocessed budgie, down.

Even though my next task was a cleanup chore of bird droppings from the bedspread, when compared to what I thought I was going to have to do, tidying up was no big undertaking. The whole time I washed away, I thanked my lucky stars both pets were safe and adamantly vowed that the bird cage door positively would be closed each time I left.

The next night when I got home I was overjoyed to hear the familiar bird sounds and feel the playful ankle attack by Comet. But the following evening, I opened the door and, as before, the entry hall was empty and the house quiet. I was certain I had closed the cage that morning so what could have happened this time?

I hurried to the family room and looked instantly at the bird cage. If I thought the drama of the other night was unusual what I saw that evening was even more unique.

Again the door was open but this time, both pets were in plain sight. Just as the lion and the lamb shall lie together, my bird and cat had decided to do likewise. Keo was on her perch chirping happily and Comet, acting as if she always had lived in a bird cage, was sprawled on the bottom of the enclosure making contented, non-threatening cat sounds.

Amazing! I watched this uncommon scene in disbelief for a few minutes before removing Comet from the cage and shutting the door. "How on earth did you get into that cage, you little rascal? Unless — of course — you've learned how to open the door!"

Comet always had a talent for opening shut objects. No closed cupboard door was too great a challenge for her agile paws. Even opening the sliding screen patio door was conquered by clawing and pulling on the screen until she had an opening big enough to get her paw into. Then, if not discovered and stopped, she would pull it open wide enough to squeeze out. Now she had added one more opening skill to her repertoire — one which I was going to have to stop.

But how had she done this new trick? I encouraged and coaxed her to open the cage. Finally convinced it was all right to show off her new accomplishment, she inched her way up the cage with her front paws while standing on her hind legs, then batted at the bar closure with her paw until it slid open.

With the door open again, Keo hopped down to the floor and the two began to play. Comet walked around the family room while Keo with a bird-waddling strut followed. Comet then ran and hid behind a door. Keo, still walking at her same pace and chirping as she went, approached the corner and out pounced the kitten, leaping so that all four paws straddled the bird yet never touched her. Obviously, they must have done this skillful maneuver before!

If the cat was going to hurt the bird, she certainly had the opportunity during the two days that they were left to their own play so I could see no reason to stop them now. I sat in the chair and watched, truly astonished at their actions and friendly relationship while at the same time, trying to decide how to safeguard the bird while I was at work.

Although the kitten was cautious with the bird, I knew Keo needed a secure place to rest out of Comet's reach when she tired of the game-playing. Definitely, I had to change the cage. If I got a cage with spaces between the bars large enough for Keo to slip through whenever she wanted and a Comet-proof latch, the bird would be free to come and go at her will.

The next day, I found such a cage and replaced the old one with the new. The bird was content with her new accommodations and in a few days, as I hoped, would go out when she wanted companionship then return to her quarters for food, water, sleep or her own playful bird needs.

With time to play when they wanted, the unlikely twosome invented several new activities that I watched as often as I could. I decided from these observations that it was the cat, not the bird, who regarded the bird as family or perhaps another funny-looking cat but no matter which, a playmate with whom she had to be careful.

Comet was the one in charge. When they played follow the leader, Comet led; when they amused themselves with hide-and-seek not only around corners and behind doors but in and out of empty boxes, the cat was the trail blazer. But by far their most unusual activity that solely depended upon Comet's wants (and one I always watched in awe), was the riding game.

Trainers for circuses, zoos or aquatic and animal parks generally teach their subjects to perform acts unusual to their natural behavior by rewarding them with a favorite food when a trick or accomplishment is performed. Through repetition and reward, the performer soon learns to respond correctly. In the case of my pets, this riding game was most unusual because they had invented, without human coaxing, a behavior not instinctive to a bird or cat with the only reward that of their own enjoyment.

To play this game, Comet would lower her tail to the floor, Keo would climb up it to her back and Comet, like a pony with rider, would give her a stroll around the room! These rides would last until Comet tired which could be anywhere from one to two minutes. Then, the cat would settle to the floor, slowly roll over on her side and Keo would waddle off onto the carpet.

I was most proud of and impressed by the talents of these two and often boasted about their remarkable relationship. During a house call to treat a sick parrot belonging to a woman who worked for a local television station, I mentioned this unusual companionship. The woman agreed they were a most unique pair and said she would tell her news staff about them.

The next day I received a phone call from Margaret Radford, a San Diego reporter for Channel 10, requesting permission to come to my home to televise a story about Keo and Comet. Naturally, most pet owners think that their pets are special, doubtlessly brighter or more clever than any other animal of the same species: I was no exception. I was thrilled and pleased to grant the interview. We scheduled the filming and as I hung up the phone, I knew it would be an exciting and eventful experience. If I had only known how it was going to be an event, I might have been less excited and more hesitant in my quick affirmative response.

Two television crewmen and a pleasant, good-humored Margaret Radford knocked on my door at the designated time. I welcomed them into the family room and the crew began pulling and tugging cords and equipment here and there while Margaret asked me questions about Keo and Comet and their friendship.

Keo stood on the floor, looking and watching the men. Comet, on the other hand, looked at them for an instant and darted into action. She attacked, jumped on and pawed the moving cords and cables like new toys brought specifically to entertain her.

The crew soon signaled they were ready to begin filming. I picked up the cat and put her next to Keo in an area the cameraman suggested.

"Play with Keo, Comet. Look Comet, here's your friend. Take her for a ride. Come, play with Keo."

Comet would not look at the bird and, as soon as I let loose of her, she ran back to the intriguing cables. No amount of coaxing, stern scolding or attempts at enticing her with her favorite toys would dissuade her from the cords even after they were in place and immobile. Again and again, I attempted to get her interested in her playmate and over and over she made a beeline back to the irresistible television equipment. The filming crew only smiled patiently.

Margaret must have sensed my frustration and tried to be reassuring. "Just give her a little time, she said. "I'm sure she'll be bored with the equipment soon."

I responded with a half-hearted, "Yeah," because I was not sure what to try next to distract the cat enough to do her much acclaimed act with a bird. I attempted several more times to get Comet interested in Keo. I tried then retried everything I could think of.

If I had trained these two to perform by a reward routine, the necessary filming doubtlessly would be completed but, with them only performing when and if they felt like it, how was I going to get them to play together? I was desperate. By now almost an hour had passed and, although the crew had been taking random footage, I knew they had nothing of real interest because it would show only an uncaged cat and bird in the same room. I knew the crew must be ready to give up at this point because I was.

"Perhaps," I said as I thought of one untried tactic, "I can get them interested in one another if I move one of their favorite playing areas, this scratching pedestal with topside bed, into the living room."

I quickly relocated it, returned for the two would-be stars, laid Comet in the bed and perched Keo on its carpeted edge. Cameras started to roll as Keo started to move. She started at the tip of the cat's tail chirping happily and strutted to the top of Comet's head while the reclining cat batted at but did not actually hit the bird with her paws. Keo played for a while with Comet's ears while Comet harmlessly pawed back at her.

I was elated and the television trio appeared relieved as frowns were traded for smiles. Although this performance was not as impressive nor did it last as long as some of their undistracted sessions, at least they had done something. The afternoon was not a complete waste of time after all.

During the next six years, Comet and Keo continued their companionship and all games except the riding

one. Because they only enjoyed pleasurable playful encounters, the pleasure of the riding game ended for Comet
about a month after it began because Keo started pulling out
tufts of Comet's hair or pinching her ears or whiskers with
her sharp beak which must have been annoying if not
painful to the cat.

    The duo never ceased to delight and astound me with
their antics. Even now, when I replay the tape of their
performance that lasted less than a minute on television and
took more than one hour to film, I am impressed with their
relationship. To me, the time that it took to shoot that very
short segment was worth it. In retrospect, however, I
wonder if the crew viewed the time involved with that
filming worthwhile. I also wonder if patience is a job re-
quirement for all television crew and reporters.

3

Animal Quips and Quirks

Most city dogs contained in fenced yards yearn for freedom and a chance to explore the outside world and will gladly escape if someone leaves a gate open. Unlike his other canine relatives, a Dalmatian with the appropriate name of Spot was the opposite and, if he were human, he would be diagnosed as having agoraphobia.

I received a phone call from his owners requesting that I come to their Pacific Beach house for a routine checkup and vaccinations. At this point, I knew nothing about him and replied, "If he isn't sick, why don't you bring Spot to me? It would save you the cost of a house call."

"Spot is not easy to take any place," he said. "In fact, I should say it's impossible. He goes berserk — runs, jumps, turns, twists and streaks off with his tail between his legs, yelping all the way. Believe me, I don't mind the additional fee you must charge because it's well worth it not to have to deal with taking him to you."

"Do you have any ideas what caused this unusual behavior?" I asked, wanting to know more about the dog's background so I could better understand and treat him.

"No, 'fraid not. We got him when he was about a year old and he has always been frantic in any place other than our back yard or inside our house."

I quickly ran through a list of possible reasons for his trauma that could be anything from being burned by a cigarette, hit by a car, kicked by someone, injured by a lawn mower or — one of hundreds of other possibilities. What-ever the unknown cause, his resulting erratic behavior that doubtlessly included an aggressive attitude towards a veterinarian, would have to be dealt with.

We agreed on a time for the next day and as I hung up, I squared my shoulders, resolute that I could handle the dog no matter what his problems were. After all, I had successfully treated many hard to handle patients before — but — just in case he would be extremely difficult — I slipped a muzzle into my medical case.

Spot was waiting in the living room when I arrived. I did what I usually do with any animal: I called him by name and stretched out my hand in a friendly manner. He came immediately to me, wagging his tail and giving my hand a wet lick while lifting his paw for me to shake it.

Although Spot may have been a prime candidate for an animal psychologist regarding some aspects of his behavior, he certainly was well-mannered with me, in fact, he was one of my most cooperative canine patients. He sat still while I ran my hands over him and even stretched out his leg for the necessary blood sample. Life as a veterinarian is definitely filled with surprises.

The term "dumb animals" originated when the word dumb meant only the inability to speak. Now, colloquially, the word means stupid and I occasionally hear this meaning used when referring to an animal. Although my patients are dumb in the sense they are unable to speak, definitely they are not dumb in the sense of being stupid. Far from it, in fact, case after case has proven to me that animals are quite perceptive, creative and anything but dumb. The mysterious lameness of Clarence, the copycat duck, reinforces my belief. I received an urgent phone call from Martha, owner of two white ducks, requesting that I come out as soon as possible because Clementine was limping. "I don't know what happened but maybe my dog got out. Taffy likes to chase the ducks and perhaps she hurt Clementine."

"Is Clarence all right?"

"Yes, he's fine. It's just Clementine."

Martha and I went to the back yard where the ducks were and the injured duck was snuggled in the grass while the other duck waddled around, looking for bugs. I picked up Clementine and ran my hands over her, feeling for anything out of the ordinary. I could find nothing so placed her back in the grass and watched as she hobbled away.

"I didn't feel any broken bones but I would like to take her in for an x-ray and run a few tests while she's there." It was possible that the duck could have gout, a common disease in birds, or perhaps it could be nutritional or something systemic in nature.

"Of course," Martha replied.

The following day, I returned with the duck and the test results. "I'm happy to tell you, all the tests were negative. I might suggest a minor nutritional adjustment but outside of that, Clementine seems to have only a sprain." As I talked, I walked the back yard looking for any holes that the duck might have stepped into and caused the sprain or places where she could have been caught and twisted her leg. I could find nothing that might be harmful. "Keep Taffy locked up," I continued, "so she can't chase the duck and aggravate that sprain and, in a week or so, she should be back to her old self."

Three days later, Martha called, quite upset. "It's Clarence. Now he's lame. He's hobbling around and favoring his left leg, exactly like Clementine did."

Good grief! It must be some kind of an epidemic. Yet, how could that be? All the tests were negative indicating that there was no transmissible disease yet — had I overlooked something? "How's Clementine? Is she better?"

"Yes. Her limp is less noticeable but Clarence — "

"I'll be there this evening as soon as the clinic closes."

We walked into the back yard while I still puzzled over this mystery and studied Clarence who was walking as if he was in as much pain as Clementine was when I first saw her. I picked him up, carefully felt his feathery body and troubled leg and discovered — nothing peculiar. I put him down and watched him limp away as if in great discomfort.

"Tell me what you have been doing and anything out of the ordinary that has happened."

"I'm absolutely positive the dog is not responsible this time because I know she has not been in the yard with the ducks. Naturally, I've spent most of my time pampering and paying attention to poor little lame Clementine. She just looked so pathetic that — " She continued on with a detailed description of each day's activities but I was not listening because she had already said something that intrigued me. What if Clarence's problem was only lack of attention? What if he was faking his hobble just to get sympathy, attention from her like she was lavishing on Clementine? I felt certain the duck was healthy so he must be feigning, putting on an act.

"I think I know what's wrong," I interrupted her. "I think you have an extremely clever duck. You've been ignoring him and he's figured out that by imitating Clementine, you'll give him more attention."

Martha was thoughtful for a moment. "You know, you may be right. I admit, I haven't been paying much attention to him."

"He certainly doesn't seem hurt or sick so why don't you try giving equal attention to both ducks. Give me a call in two or three days and let me know how they're acting."

Martha's report confirmed what I had suspected: Clarence's "lame duck" act was disappearing rapidly now that she was giving him as much attention as Clementine. His charade was hardly dumb, in fact, I think his strategy was quite resourceful and most effective.

Another case of an animal getting attention when it desired occurred with Ham, my white and rusty-orange short-haired hamster. Cuddly hamsters are popular pets for people living in close quarters because they are small and require a minimum of space, are easy to take care of and extremely clean animals who groom their coats often. They are adventuresome, investigative, delight in carrying things in their mouths, love to chew on objects and provide owners with many entertaining hours because of their antics.

Ham, true to his hamster nature, enjoyed roaming through the numerous trails in his cage and exploring the house when in his clear plastic hamster ball that protected him from the batting and pouncing of curious cats. He also liked to be held and petted by anyone but particularly by my son Lop. It was this combination of exploring and his affection for Lop that caused him to devise an unusual behavior.

Like most teenagers, Lop spent a great deal of time in his room with the door shut which meant he was ignoring Ham. Ham, who obviously did not like this, soon discovered a creative way to get Lop's attention. He would roll the ball down the hall, stop in front of the door and then rock the ball back and forth, hitting it against Lop's door which made a noise almost as loud as a knock. Lop would open the door and Ham got the reward he wanted — to spend time with and be petted by Lop.

Clive, the basset hound, was owned by a physician and his wife who had no children. They had raised him since he was a puppy, treating him as though he was their child, pampering and spoiling him thoroughly. But things were to change dramatically for Clive because Linda was pregnant.

After the baby was born, Bob and Linda were busy caring for the needs of the baby and poor Clive was slighted, not intentionally but there simply were not enough hours in the day to give equal time to the dog and the baby.

Clive was upset by this lack of attention and in retaliation, would jump up on the couple's bed and defecate and urinate on the bedspread as if to say, "This is where it happened and I don't like it." Naturally Bob and Linda were beside themselves, disappointed with Clive's behavior and frustrated by wondering how to stop his disgusting act.

I suggested that, first, they put a sheet of plastic over the bed and try very hard to give more affection and time to Clive. If after a short period of time that did not work, I would give them a repellent that the dog would find offensive but would not bother them. If that did not work, the last suggestion I had was to call in a behavioral specialist.

Only step one was necessary. By the end of a week, Clive had stopped his repulsive behavior and was acting his usual self.

Fred, like most yellow-naped Amazon parrots, was lime green with yellow across the nape, red on the outermost wing feathers and about twelve-inches long, and lived in a lovely home in La Mesa. His cage was usually kept by the back door but because the owners decided to add on a large deck, he was moved to a nearby room in an alcove opposite the construction side of the house. The new house extension and deck took about one month for the noisy workmen to finish.

About two weeks after the job was completed and because it was time for Fred's annual checkup, Ann called me to come out. I rang the door bell and Ann ushered me in. Good heavens! What a commotion. It sounded as though a full work crew was busy hammering, sawing and drilling with both hand and power tools.

"I thought you had finished your house construction?"

"We have," Ann said. "That's not workmen, it's Fred. He's learned all the sounds he heard while the construction was going on. We thought we had moved him far enough away from the noise but obviously not. He's driving all of us crazy. What on earth can we do to "unlearn" the sounds he's learned?"

I listened to his repertoire of noises. He did an excellent job of mimicking all the tools but I was particularly impressed with his version of a drill because it is a difficult sound for a bird to make.

"He's really quite good, isn't he?" I smiled, staring in the direction of the bird's room. "I guess you should be grateful he wasn't close enough to hear the off-colored language the workmen were probably using. You know how easily bird's pick up new words, especially four letter ones — "

Whoops! I looked at Ann. Obviously what I said was not what she wanted to hear because she had her arms folded across her chest and looked at me with disgust.

"Perhaps, in time, the newness will wear off and he'll become bored with those noises." Ann still looked displeased.

"Well, it's very difficult to "untrain" a bird but you can try to teach him new sounds that are pleasant to hear. You might turn the radio on to classical music or, perhaps, get some records of other birds singing or talking." These suggestions must have been what she was hoping for be-cause, at last, she smiled.

Although Fred never completely forgot his tool sounds, with time he did learn other phrases, words and songs and would intersperse them with his annoying hammer, saw or drill imitation. At least now the owners heard a variety of sounds rather a monotonous all-day-long serenade of harsh noises.

Barney was a one-year-old basset hound with a most indiscriminate appetite: When his owners took him for a walk, he would devour any loose object in his path, whether edible or not. Because of this unique eating habit,

I saw him frequently always with the same symptoms of diarrhea and vomiting as he tried to expel the foreign substances that did not agree with him.

"So far, you — and Barney — have been fortunate because he hasn't eaten anything that has caused truly serious problems and because you have brought him in quickly for medical treatment. However," I warned, "for his well-being, you must muzzle him when taking him for a walk to prevent him from swallowing something poisonous or sharp that could puncture his intestines."

"We will, Doctor. I just keep thinking that each time we bring him in feeling so miserable certainly this time he's learned that if he eats weird things, he'll feel awful and won't do it again." She sighed. "I guess not."

About four months passed before I saw Barney again with the usual vomiting and diarrhea but, in addition, that afternoon he was obviously in great discomfort. I ran my hands over his stomach and felt a hard mass. He definitely had an obstruction of some kind.

I peered over my glasses and asked, "Do you have any idea what he ate this time?"

"No," Marion said, twisting the tissue in her hand. "We took him for a walk this morning — and — I guess he picked up something. He — he didn't have his muzzle on," she stammered. I could see puddles of tears welling in her eyes. "I'm so sorry. It's all my fault. Will he be all right?"

"I'll do my best." I picked up the lethargic fifty-pound hound and took him into the x-ray room, placed him on the table and looked at him. He definitely was feeling poorly. It seemed his floppy ears drooped more than usual and his soulful brown eyes were dulled by pain. "You really did it this time, didn't you Barney, old pal." He feebly wagged his tail.

The film showed what I had felt; a round, solid mass in the intestinal tract. Although I still had no clue as to what it was, it was obvious that the only way Barney was going to get rid of this blockage was through immediate surgery.

All the while I was preparing him for the operation, I wondered what I would find. Knowing Barney's appetite for any and everything, I could not even venture a logical guess what the blockage might be.

I cut into the troubled area, opened the intestine and stared in disbelief. No wonder he had a stomach ache. He had swallowed three indigestible smooth, round — not pebbles — but rocks! The biggest one, the one that was causing the major problem, was larger than a golf ball but smaller than a tennis ball and the other two were about the size of agate marbles.

I removed them and as I sutured him, could not help chuckling over this amazing hound whose mother must have mated with a vacuum cleaner to produce such an offspring. To ingest these objects, he had to sniff so vigorously with his mouth open that he would suck up anything that happened to be in his path as efficiently as any household vacuum.

After I showed the owners what Barney had eaten, assured them that surgery went well and he should be fine, they in turn assured me about Barney. "We've learned our lesson. Barney will NEVER be outside without a muzzle."

As any veterinarian will tell you, unusual cases abound and an animal doctor needs to not only administer the proper medication and its dosage but also be able to trouble shoot problems that are rarely or sometimes never found in textbooks. Common sense combined with a Sherlock Holmes ability for deductive reasoning become a necessity when dealing with baffling cases.

Toni brought in her lime green, double yellow-headed Amazon parrot, a bird similar in looks to the yellow-naped but with yellow extending from the head down onto the neck and upper breast, for a routine check and blood test. I discovered it had a slight increase in the number of yeast organisms in the crop that, although the bird was not in any real danger, I wanted the condition controlled before it became a problem. I prescribed a medication that I had used previously with success.

"Add a few drops of this to Zeke's drinking water for fourteen days. The medicine will turn the water a bright blue but the taste of it won't be changed enough to be unpalatable."

Three days later, Toni called to say that there was no problem regarding Zeke drinking his medicated water, in fact, it was quite the opposite. He was drinking excessive amounts of it which meant his droppings were very wet and messy. What could she do to correct this?

"Can you bring him back today and let me take another look at him?" What could be causing this abnormal thirst? Had I overlooked something?

A thorough recheck of the bird later that day showed no other diseases or illnesses. "Discontinue the medicine for a few days and let's see what he does. Please call and let me know how he's doing."

Two days later, Toni called to say that without the medicine in the water, he was drinking his normal amount of water. "Good," I replied, still uncertain as to why he had drunk so much water before but delighted that he was back to a regular drinking pattern. "I want to control the yeast organisms so try adding the medicine to the water again."

Two days later, Toni called to say he was again drinking great quantities of water. "What now?" she asked, her frustration obvious by her clipped, emphatic pronunciation of the question.

I wish I knew. I swirled around in my desk chair and stared out the window, pensively rubbing my chin. What could possibly be causing Zeke to drink so much? Actually he should not be aware of the medicine in the water except for the fact that —

"I have an idea. Perhaps Zeke is attracted to the color of his water so let's try something. For the next two days, don't put the medicine in but add a few drops of blue food coloring to duplicate the color of the medicine. Call me and let me know how he reacts to that."

Toni phoned back with Zeke's update: He was again drinking excessive amounts of water. "Well," I laughed, "looks like Zeke likes — really likes — the color blue. I'll prescribe another medication and this time it won't be blue."

If one is allergic to dogs and cats but loves animals such as Randy and Sherry Lane did, what animal would make a good household pet? A friend suggested they check into getting a duck.

They went to a pet store to look at a brood of downy mallard ducks and, as soon as one of the ducklings saw them, it immediately ran towards them. Randy picked up the one and one-half ounce baby and it snuggled close. With the mutual love-at-first-sight rapport that happened between the three of them and a fee of $5.95, Hobie had a new home and owners. As the days went by, Hobie became a beloved and integral part of their family and a duck who developed a must unique and baffling problem, one I had never before encountered.

The Lanes brought Hobie to me when the duckling was about three months old because she was having what they called "seizures." These seizures only occurred after they had been gone for a period of time and then when they returned, as soon as Hobie saw them, she would immediately go down on the floor, stretch out her neck, hold her body rigid and pass out.

"I'm truly concerned — and worried. Hobie is a wonderful pet that we both love tremendously. What could possibly be wrong?" Randy asked.

Could Hobie's condition be caused by a central nervous system disorder? Or, I thought, perhaps it is a nutritional deficiency or — no use trying to guess until I knew some facts about her physical condition. "At this point, I can't give even an educated guess. Let me run some tests."

The results that I had hoped would give me the answer to her strange behavior only showed she had a mild calcium deficiency, a relatively minor item when it came to diagnosing the reasons for her seizures. Although I did not find any evidence regarding a central nervous system disorder, there was a possibility she was reacting to something in or on the backyard grass where she played.

"Hello, Randy. Doctor Ewing here. I have some good news. Hobie seems to be a very healthy duck except for a slight calcium deficiency which a diet supplementation should correct."

"That's great! But what about her seizures?"

"Well, I'm afraid I still don't know. However, have

you sprayed your yard recently with any type of insecticide?"

"Yes, a few weeks ago. Do you think that might be the cause?"

"It could be that she's allergic to something in the spray. I suggest you hose the yard thoroughly to get rid of as much of its residue as possible. Then keep Hobie inside for a few days and let's see if that makes a difference."

Two weeks passed before I heard from Randy again. "We hosed the yard, kept Hobie in as you suggested but she's still having her fainting spells when I come home."

"Hmm," I muttered while quickly thinking of what to do next. "Perhaps she's allergic to something she's eating. Let's change her diet slightly." I suggested a different combination of foods with more emphasis on those with extra protein, calcium, essential vitamins, minerals and fatty acids. "Watch for any changes after you've made the food changes and call me frequently with a report of her condition whether there are changes or not."

The conversations with Randy throughout the following months indicated that Hobie was still having seizures. I continued suggesting dietary changes, had Hobie into the clinic for more routine tests and even kept her overnight for observation. During this stay, I allowed her to roam the clinic so I could watch her and, I hoped, see one of her seizures for myself and also because she enjoyed her freedom and being with people: She followed us from room to room as we performed our duties, quacking with pleasure as she waddled.

However, during those two days, she never had a seizure and I still had not seen one of these extraordinary behaviors described by her owners. I had run every test, tried everything I knew to unravel this mystery but, until I could see one of her fainting spells, I knew of nothing else to do. I was truly stymied. I assured the Lanes that Hobie was healthy and that these spells — whatever they were — were not life-threatening. I sent her home with Sherry, still mystified by the unique behavior detailed by the owners.

Several month later, Randy called, informing me that Hobie had laid an egg every other day for twenty-one days. "Is this normal?" he asked, as worried as any child's parent.

"Yes, there's no problem there and obviously she's not extremely calcium deficient or she wouldn't be able to lay eggs. Has there been any change or is she still having seizures?"

"Yes," he said, "just as she always has, whenever I am gone for a while, return and she sees me."

I sighed and shook my head. "Why don't you bring her in so I can check her calcium level after all that egg laying and run some other diagnostic procedures. Perhaps I'll find something this time that might indicate the reason for her spells."

Again, I tested Hobie for everything imaginable. Again, the results showed only a mild calcium deficiency and, again, I had no inkling about what caused her seizures. I sent her home, perplexed and somewhat disappointed with myself that I could not find a reason for the bizarre behavior that so far, I had not seen.

A few months later, Randy called to ask if he could board Hobie at the clinic for four or five days because they had to go out of town. "Of course," I replied. "And maybe by being able to observe her for several days, I'll learn something about her condition."

The Lanes arrived with Hobie and — just like a popular commercial on television that states: "If only a baby came with an owner's manual" — well, Hobie did. The loving owners had compiled a four page, single-spaced, typed reference guide detailing information about their cherished pet. Without a doubt, this was one of the most complete guides for the care and feeding of a pet I have ever seen, entitled, "Just a little bit about the duck I love."

In the section headed Hobie's Favorite Food, were: parrot scratch (with seed shells removed), spaghetti (in water, no butter or sauce please), live feeder fish, snails, earthworms, ice plant, little red Spanish peanuts, sunflower seeds (no shells), sometimes likes peas, rice, various meats and cantaloupe.

The lengthy part on water included making sure there was ample water for drinking — "She takes food out of the dish and dunks it into the water like dunking doughnuts in coffee; bathing — should take a full bath at least once a day." The half page about feathers explained her behavior during molting and how best to pick her up to avoid hurting her during this time.

The most interesting section to me or anyone who is interested in animal behavior was called "Hobie Habits,

Specialties and Things To Know." Because I think the information from the Lanes is so interesting, I have included it below, just as they wrote it.

"She is routine in her behavior. For the most part, this is good, and at worst, interesting. If we come home from work with fish for her, then the next night when we get home, she will be expecting us to again bring fish.

One day she decided that she wanted to lay her egg on the family room carpet where I had been sitting, instead of in her house where she always does. Despite the fact that we didn't let her lay it there, for the next three mornings she insisted on going over to that spot to lay. She finally got the hint.

When Hobie is relaxed and having fun, some of the more direct responses that she gives are:

Kiss — usually by request, sometimes she will initiate

Bye-bye — means she gets to go for a car ride

Up duck — she helps us pick her up

Gather the duck — She will put on a display of protest. We do this to let her know that we are going to bring an end to her play time (such as swimming or mud grubbing) and put her in her outside house. This doesn't work at bedtime because she likes to go to bed. Her bedtime excitement is triggered by our actions. Her associations include the preparation of her food from the kitchen, our shredding newspapers for her nest, and us turning off the computer which plays *Lullaby and Good Night.* If all of these things happen within the same time frame, she will race back and forth between the kitchen and her bed until we have it all ready for her.

Other actions include:

If she stands close by and looks at you, she wants to be held.

If she stands next to you and pecks at the back of your leg, she wants to be fed.

Bobbing her head up and down while clucking over and over again indicates that she is uncomfortable. This can come from being hungry, needing some exercise or from wanting to get rid of an egg. Figuring it out is usually a process of elimination. If she isn't laying (like now), it won't be an egg bothering her, so when is the last time she ate or took a walk? Occasionally she will also do this if she doesn't like the music we are playing.

She sometimes watches TV, especially shows with airplanes.

In General:

When she isn't laying, she is more spirited, playful and gets real "goosey" sometimes. Her favorite things to play with are soft foam bedroom slippers and socks if they have colors and patterns that appeal to her. She seldom plays with things on her own; she likes someone to participate. Often she will instigate the play by biting at the item, and although it is just play, her biting can be vigorous and leave welts where the skin is not protected. One other word of caution, sometimes when she gets that spirited look in her eyes, she may pretend you have bugs on your body and try to pick them off — like freckles or scabs or moving eyelashes can be a great target. Usually a long loving look into your eyes is a give away for this move.

She normally does not walk around something that is only a few inches high; she will walk on it or through it instead.

Shadows frighten her, and she might completely lose it at the sight of a regular sponge mop.

One honk — she feels threatened by a predator (dogs, cats, etc., and sometimes unrealistically, birds that fly too close to her).

A loud honk with several less loud ones to follow — she is calling to us to come and be a companion. She will often do this in the evening when one of us leaves her presence, or when we are walking up to the house after being gone.

Summary: Hobie likes water and people in that order. She is a fussy eater. Her balance is not that great so don't leave her alone in high places where she might fall or try to jump. Please make sure she has plenty of her calcium and vitamin supplements. Hobie has not laid now for about two weeks.

Nicknames: Sweetheart, Quackers, Queeki Queeki

Hope you enjoy her companionship half as much as we do. Thanks for looking out after her."

Indeed, this duck was loved and cared about by her owners! And, I and my staff certainly knew without experimenting what she liked and disliked. Now, if during this time I could see one of her seizures, maybe I could solve the mystery.

Each day, I hoped would be the day when she would have an attack while I was there, however, each day passed without such an event. That afternoon, Randy came to pick up Hobie. We chatted for a few moments in the reception room and then walked back to the animal cage area. Hobie, who had been wandering the halls spied her beloved owner and immediately plopped on the floor, pulling her wings close to her side as she stretched out rigidly. Her eyes were not quite closed indicating that she had not entirely passed out.

"There! Look at that! That's what she does only this time she didn't completely faint like she usually does. What do you make of it?" He started towards her.

"Stop! Don't touch her yet." My mind raced as I observed the helpless-looking duck spread out on the linoleum. "When she has one of these fits, what do you do?"

"I go to her quickly, caress her while I talk lovingly to her and then pick her up. Why? Shouldn't I do that?"

I studied the immobile duck and in her prone position which — suggested a sexually submissive duck posture! That was it! As a duckling, she had imprinted on Randy and, as she matured sexually, to show her wholehearted affection to the male in her life, she used this instinctive behavior to display it! In addition, when she had a seizure, Randy in return showered her with what she wanted; instant attention and affection. Undoubtedly, the reason she had not passed out totally this time was because she was not at home. The still unfamiliar sounds and surroundings had distracted her from being completely overcome by the sight of Randy.

I laughed and Randy looked at me with a mixture of puzzlement and concern. "Relax, Randy, good news. I know why Hobie has these mysterious seizures and, as I suspected originally, there is nothing physically wrong and most assuredly, these attacks are not life-threatening. Hobie is simply in love with you."

To Call or not to Call

I always encourage bird owners to call me immediately if a pet is not as perky as usual or is doing something out of the ordinary. Birds tend to suppress symptoms of a disease or problem so if unusual behavior is not called to the attention of a veterinarian when first noted, it can mean that the necessary medication and treatment may be administered too late and the bird may die. An observant bird owner can make the difference between life and death for his or her beloved pet. Because of these factors, I often received middle-of-the-evening phone calls and frequently made late-night house calls.

Bob and Jane purchased their first bird, a young yellow-naped Amazon parrot, inexpensively because he had been smuggled in from Mexico. Because they knew that any bird with an unknown background or without a medical certificate should be taken to a veterinarian for a complete checkup as soon as possible, they brought him to me. My findings showed he was gravely ill.

Like other owners who buy illegal birds, what they may have saved in the purchase price would be spent for the necessary medical treatment to return the bird to good health. The stressful way a bird is caught, the conditions in which it is transported — generally, in quarters so cramped the bird cannot move, has no food or water and, because of the proximity to other birds that are sick, catches a disease — means a smuggled bird usually is ill.

Unfortunately, bird smuggling is a common and lucrative business. The restrictions of the Mexican government concerning exporting birds and those of the United States regarding importing them make it extremely difficult to get a bird across the border legally. These regulations also prevent aviculturists in the States from establishing breeding stock of sufficient quality and quantity. In addition, as the forests of Mexico and Central and South America are cut and the habitat of the birds is destroyed, their numbers are dwindling — making them even more desirable as a sought-after commodity to the smuggler. Because of this limited supply and the growing demand, unless the export and import rules are changed, in all probability, soon all species of Amazon parrots could be on the endangered species list.

In order to survive, Rex, like other illegal birds I had examined, required constant care. During the past several months, Bob and Jane had hand-fed him, given him injections and antibiotics and, regulated the humidity and maintained the temperature of eighty-five to ninety-five degrees in his environment. Finally, this around-the-clock treatment was paying off because he was starting to improve.

Because they were deeply concerned with Rex's health, Bob called me to ask if I thought Rex was now well enough for them to leave him alone overnight because they needed to check on their property in Los Angeles. I told them I thought so and merely to keep the bird in its cage with the heat on and ample food and water.

A few days later, my phone rang and I barely had time to say hello when a most anxious voice blurted out, "I think you better come over immediately, Doctor Ewing. Rex is acting like he's having convulsions. We shouldn't have left him. Please, come quickly!"

"Bob, is that you?" I inquired in a soothing manner. Although I recognized his voice and the bird's name, I was hoping to calm him down.

"Oh, yes. Sorry. I'm just so worried."

"Tell me exactly what's happening. Describe what Rex is doing."

"It's awful," he said, his voice wavering. "He must be in a great deal of pain or having some horrible attack. His head is bobbing up and down and he's swaying from side to side — really fast — on his perch."

A smile trickled across my face and I chuckled. "I don't think Rex's problem is serious, in fact, what he's doing is a normal bird reaction. He's happy to have you both home and is simply anxious for you to hold him, to give him some affection. Go pick him up, love him a bit, and I bet he'll settle down. Call me back if that doesn't calm him but I feel certain he's perfectly fine."

I knew that I wouldn't be hearing from Bob again that day. Because until the last few weeks the bird always had been sick, they never knew how a healthy, normal bird acts when its happy to have its owners come home.

Another concerned bird owner who followed my advice called me late at night, almost in hysterics. "You — you must come over." She sounded as if she were attempting to dam a deluge of tears. "Something's — terribly — wrong with Sarah," she choked out the sentence.

"What seems to be the problem?"

"She can't stay on her perch, she keeps falling off. I'm afraid she must be sick. Please, come quickly."

"Yes, of course, I'll be there in about twenty minutes."

Indeed, she was correct in calling because this bird might have a severe problem. As I hung up the phone I mentally raced through all the possibilities of what falling from a perch might mean. It could indicate something as serious as a central nervous system disorder, lead poisoning, a calcium deficiency found in seed-eating birds because their diet is not supplemented properly, a liver disease that causes a toxic buildup or an ear infection that affects the equilibrium. It could be something less hard to deal with such as a sore leg or a previous injury or even simply falling off its perch which many birds do occasionally.

This bird was a young, less than five-years-old, double yellow-headed Amazon parrot. By observing my Amazon as well as others, I knew Amazons are fairly clumsy and tend to fall off perches more often than other birds. Why, I'm not sure but I suspect they may have dreams that cause them to fall. If a bird slips from a tree, it has time to catch itself and fly back to a branch; however, in a cage, there's no time to recover so it can hit the cage floor with enough force to receive an injury.

I got dressed, checked to make sure I had medication with me for any of the possible illnesses or happenings and, as I drove to her apartment, ran through this bird's history. I had examined and tested Sarah only a few months before and she had no problems at that time. There was nothing in her medical profile that could help me with the reason why she was falling off a perch.

I barely tapped my knuckles against the door and Mary opened it. Her eyes were swollen and red and her forehead tight with concern.

"Oh, thanks for coming so quickly. I'm — I'm just frantic." She wrung her hands as she paced the floor.

"Let's have a look. It's possible it's nothing more than an accidental fall off the perch," I said, trying to comfort her. "Have you ever seen her fall before?" I walked towards the far end of the kitchen and dining area where Sarah and her large wrought iron bird cage were located.

"No. Never," she replied.

I picked up the green and yellow bird, talking re-assuringly to her as I ran my hands over her body, touching areas where she might be enlarged or tender that would give a reflexive "ouch" response from her. Nothing. No sign of anything wrong. I rechecked her again then put her back on the perch.

"Well," I said, "I can't find anything. She seems quite healthy to me. You've never seen her fall, right?"

"That's right. I just hear a loud noise, run in to see what's happened and she's on the bottom of the cage, shaking herself. I don't understand it."

Frankly, neither did I. "There's nothing I can do tonight because she seems all right. If she continues to fall off her perch, give me another call and I'll reexamine her."

We walked into the living room, out of sight of the bird. I sat on the couch still puzzled by what may have caused the bird to fall and making notes while Mary went into another room to get her checkbook.

Crash! The bird had fallen again.

I leaped up, crept to the corner of the room and peeked around the doorway just far enough to see but not far enough to call attention to myself. Sure enough, Sarah was shaking herself off, ruffling her feathers and slowly climbing back to her perch. What had happened? Why had she fallen?

I watched from my hiding place, barely daring to breathe for fear of distracting her. Sarah, now back on her perch, sat still for a few seconds then started rocking her body to and fro, building up momentum as she moved. Then, up she jumped, did a somersault in the air and slammed down onto the bottom of the cage.

No wonder there was such a racket. Even a bird weighing less than a pound when throwing its whole body weight with such force can make quite a noise when ricocheting off an amplifying metal sounding board!

I observed as again she did the same acrobatic routine. Obviously, she enjoyed this activity and had learned how to jump and crash-land without hurting herself otherwise she would not continue with the game. I now had a diagnosis. I grinned, once more pleased by the creativity of birds who never have ceased to amaze me with their individualistic behavior patterns and unique actions.

Mary scurried back. "I heard that! What's wrong?"

"Sh," I said, putting a finger to my lips. "Watch."

Again, the feathered performer trouped into action while Mary looked with wide eyes, shaking her head. "I don't believe it," she whispered. "That little squirt."

We both laughed aloud. Sarah, now back on her perch and undoubtedly ready to tumble again, heard us and looked over instantly. With people watching, she stood still, eyed us for a few seconds, then began preening herself as if nothing out of the ordinary had happened.

"There is, I'm delighted to say, absolutely nothing wrong with her. Because she never does that trick when anyone is watching her tells me that she has created a game to entertain herself when she's bored. You've nothing to worry about. You just have an inventive bird.

"However, to protect her from possible injuries, you might want to pad the cage and keep toys out of her jumping zone."

"Indeed I will," she replied, grinning with a smile so broad that it almost stretched from ear to ear.

A Peck of Trouble

The beauty of a peacock strutting about while fanning its exquisite, iridescent blue and green tail is an admirable sight. Many people keep peacocks for this elegance and because they are friendly pets that provide a burglar alarm system: When disturbed, they cry out a noisy shriek. As patients, they are docile and rarely jab their beaks with enough force to pierce the skin but, they still can be a peck of trouble for a veterinarian.

Nero, one of ten peacocks owned by Betty Henderson, was her favorite. She called the day before requesting that I come out because Nero had "something wrong with his neck." From her brief description, I could not make even an educated guess at what was wrong and, more perplexing, it did not sound like any condition I had run across before.

The day was warm, sunny and the hour and one-half ride to the Henderson ranch in San Diego county delightful. The swirling dust behind the motor home must have alerted Betty I was arriving because she was standing in front of the ranch house as I drove up.

"Hi, Doctor Ewing," she yelled. "I'm glad you could make it today. I know it's a long trip but I think it's necessary.

"No problem." I grabbed my medical bag and stepped out of the RV. "The drive here is always a pleasant change of pace from my city calls and, from what you told me, I couldn't diagnose or recommend a treatment for Nero without coming out to see him."

We headed towards the peacock pens. "Is he eating and acting like he usually does?"

"Yes. He seems to feel all right but he looks so strange. I don't know if he'll be okay without medical treatment or if he needs your help. I thought you better take a look at him and tell me what should be done."

By now we were in front of the pen but Nero was looking towards the back of it so I could not yet see his neck. I entered the cage and slowly walked around to face him. "You said — " I gasped.

Nero was an incredible sight. About six to eight inches of his neck skin had been stripped, pushed down from below his head to his shoulders, leaving dry, crusty, red tissue exposed. The now compressed skin at the base of his neck was folded into wrinkled layers making him look like he was wearing a turtleneck sweater!

"Well," I muttered, glancing at the chicken wire enclosure with spaces big enough for a playful bug-searching peacock to get his head through then have difficulty getting it out. "Looks like Nero got his head stuck in the fence and peeled back the neck skin while trying to get loose."

I reached around and held him in the corner so I could more clearly see his raw neck. The tissue needed to be covered with some kind of bandage because if left without an outer layer, like an untreated wound, infection would set in easily. He would not survive without a protective covering.

"I'm afraid I'll have to take him to the hospital. I don't have the correct medical supplies or bandages with me," I said while at the same time wondering exactly what those items would be.

"Oh, dear! Is it serious? I love him so. Will he be all right?"

"Yes, it's serious," I replied to her first question. I hesitated before answering her second one because I never had seen, let alone treated, a bird in this condition and to make matters worse, I did not know of another veterinarian who had, so informative consultation would be improbable. At this point, I was not sure how to save the life of this stately bird.

"I'll do everything I possibly can for Nero." I tried to sound reassuring. "I'll know more after I give him a thorough exam and run some tests. I'll call you as soon as I know something."

"All right," she replied solemnly. "I have a large box you can use to carry him in. Let — let me help you get him in it and carry him to the RV." She wiped a tear from the corner of her eye.

I waved goodbye and headed towards San Diego, so engrossed with Nero and his problem, the return drive seemed to take only a few minutes. I parked the motor home and carried the peacock and container into the examination room. Doctor Carlos Gonzales, a veterinarian and business partner at that time, walked into the room.

"Take a look at this," I said as I removed the bird and placed him on the examining table. "What do you think can be done?"

Carlos scrutinized Nero. "I'm not sure. Could you pull the skin back up and stitch it?"

I reexamined the bird, touching the pouchy folds. "No, it's been too long since he had this accident. The tissue is too dry, too shrunk, to pull up."

Doctor Gonzales shook his head, mumbled "You get the damnedest cases," and left to examine his canine patient. I stared at Nero a few minutes then retreated to my office where perhaps a solution existed in one of my numerous medical textbooks. I thumbed through each volume and read every paragraph that might have an answer or even a clue about what to do. Nothing. Absolutely nothing that pertained to Nero's circumstances.

I swiveled around in my desk chair and stared out the window. Nero, like a human with severe burns, required a protective covering to allow the tissue time to regenerate. What if I treated him the same way? During my military tour, I served as the director of medical civil defense for the Defense Civil Preparedness Agency in the Pentagon. One of the products that I and other associates developed was a synthetic skin covering for nuclear weapon burns. The material was designed to cover the burned area and form a matrix that allowed skin to grow between the remaining microscopic viable skin cells and, at the same time, stimulated growth. Testing proved that this material worked well on the human epidermis but, would it work on a bird that had lost not only skin but feathers?

It was worth trying and — it was the only probable solution to Nero's dilemma I could think of. I turned back to my desk, immediately phoned the Pentagon for the names and phone numbers of those currently working on the project then contacted them.

By 10 a.m. the next day, I had the requested package of Epi-lock®. Carlos and I took Nero into surgery as soon as possible, anesthetized him, removed the dead tissue and applied the material as directed. Now came the tough part; waiting the necessary ten days while wondering if the material was working and not being able to lift the bandages to see if it was. If I removed the wrapping too soon, cell regeneration could be destroyed, ruining any progress that I hoped was occurring.

Nero ate and slept well during the required waiting period. The medical dressing did not seem to bother him, in fact, he ignored it and acted as if he always had worn a pliable, whitish collar; however, because of the weight of it, he did have to get into some awkward and peculiar-looking positions in order to maintain his balance.

Finally, the day arrived to return the peacock to surgery and remove the dressing. Carlos and I carefully unwrapped the material and peeled it back, anxious to see what was happening underneath.

His neck was an amazing, colorful sight that looked like a scene from a science fiction movie. There were off-white strands of connective tissue, yellowish fat, bluish veinoles, reddish arterioles and capillaries, all glistening and damp because of the healing process. Epi-lock® was working.

I beamed with pleasure as we wrapped his neck with a new dressing and, as soon as I could, called Betty to tell her the good news. "Nero will be home in no time at all," I proudly promised. "Before he returns, however, you should replace his fence with a different sized chicken wire so he won't do this again."

Nero recovered better than I even hoped he would. In about three months, his skin had grown back, the follicles regenerated and feathers grew in every place except an area about the size of a quarter under his chin. His accident and treatment were so unique, the Association of Avian Veterinarians asked us to present a paper about this case at their 1987 meeting in Hawaii. To my knowledge, we were the first veterinarians to do this procedure and we may be the only ones who have done such an operation. I have yet to hear any colleague discuss a case like Nero's — nor for that matter, describe any long-necked bird that looked like he was wearing a turtleneck sweater.

Buzzie's rearing was as unusual as the medical treatment he required. Most people get birds when they are young but not as young as this peacock because he was still in the shell. Robert Buzikowski, an assistant head keeper at the San Diego Zoo, gave the egg — white and slightly larger than a chicken egg — to Jeanette Simpson and her son Burt to hatch and the grateful couple named the hatched bird after him, Buzzie.

From the incubator, to hand-feeding him with chicken mash starter for the next two to three weeks, the twosome worked with him diligently until he was able to eat on his own. As Buzzie matured, he endeared himself to his owners by his unique personality and actions that sometimes were comical. Like most peacocks, he faithfully clucked a warning whenever a guest or stranger appeared but, unlike other peacocks, he loved to be petted on the forehead. On a hot summer day, he figured out how to beat the heat by standing in his water bowl. Whenever Jeanette came home from an errand, she would go to her bedroom window and call out "hello" to Buzzie in his pen. In response, he would cackle and fan his exquisite tail for her to admire while strutting about. They were proud and extremely fond of their elegant bird.

Buzzie was about eleven years old when Burt called me to their home in Poway because the peacock was not eating properly and he suspected the bird was sick. I looked him over and decided that he must have ingested a foreign substance and had an intestinal blockage. I needed to x-ray him to find out if and where the blockage actually existed.

Because I did not yet have my fully equipped Bird Center, I took him to a clinic where I had privileges. After the x-rays were developed, a staff veterinarian and I agreed that a blockage was visible in the digestive tract, a delicate area in which to work in any animal but particularly in a bird. The surgery to clean out the area would not be easy and there were no guarantees that Buzzie would survive; however, without the surgery, he was certain to die.

I called Doctor Philip Ensley, an experienced and knowledgeable San Diego Zoo veterinarian, told him about Buzzie's situation and he asked that I bring the peacock to the zoo. Phil examined the bird, x-rayed him again and concurred that surgery was necessary. Phil offered to assist and suggested the operation be performed as soon as possible at the zoo hospital. I was surprised by his offer to use the zoo facilities because generally only zoo animals are treated here. Phil must have noticed my somewhat amazed look.

"It only seems proper to do the surgery here," he replied, a smile crossing his face, "since the peacock egg came from the zoo, it seems that we have a responsibility to help the bird survive, especially since the owners named the peacock after one of our keepers."

I called the owners, explained Buzzie's condition and the risks involved to remove the blockage and requested permission to perform the surgery.

"I understand," Burt said, "and I want him to have the best chance for survival. He is one of the best pets we've ever had. Yes, please do whatever is necessary to help him."

"Because of the urgency of his situation," I continued, "we will be operating almost immediately. If you wish, you can watch the surgery from the viewing window above the operating room."

"We're leaving right now," Burt replied.

Phil, I and a qualified staff person held Buzzie on the table while anesthesia was given through a cone mask over his beak. After he was asleep, we transferred him to a surgical table, intubated and placed him on anesthetic gas. The assistant prepared Buzzie for surgery by removing the downy feathers in the abdominal region and scrubbing the surgical site.

Doctor Ensley made the incision and we located and cautiously removed the blockage shown on the x-rays. But, once the area was opened and visible, we discovered another problem in an area more delicate than the one in which we were working: the gizzard. Buzzie's impaction extended into his gizzard.

The gizzard, a heavy muscle with a pleated interior lining and a thick, leathery outer covering, acts as a food grinder and is common to avian species. Because of its structure, surgery on a gizzard is rare and challenging. Any time this area is cut into, it is extremely difficult to suture it to prevent leakage into the abdominal cavity. If leakage occurs, infection — peritonitis — sets in and the patient usually dies. None of the few gizzard surgeries I had done had been successful.

Phil looked at me at the same time as I looked at him over the rim of my glasses. Each of us shook our heads and sighed, fully aware of the unfavorable odds of successfully operating on a gizzard but knowing it was necessary. Our patient's chance for survival was poor.

"We have no choice," Phil said. "We've got to open the gizzard to correct the problem."

A wave of sadness swept over me as I glanced up to the observation area and saw Jeanette and Burt watching. I was grateful they could not see my long face under the surgical mask.

We proceeded, carefully removing the heavy fibrous material blocking the gizzard. Next came the critical suturing. We stitched, checking and double-checking, to make sure the incision was as completely closed as possible.

As soon as I could, I joined a worried Jeanette and Burt and told them what we found and the corrective surgery done. "The operation, technically speaking, went well but we won't know if it is a true success for several days. Buzzie will need careful monitoring and medication for the next few days so I'm taking him home with me when he's ready to travel."

I made a pen for him out of cardboard boxes, put it in the garage and placed him in it. For the next two days, Buzzie took his oral and injected medicine without objection and seemed perky and alert. Best of all, by the third day, he showed no signs of an infection. I called Phil, anxious to tell him how well Buzzie was doing and that we had succeeded. The pleasure and excitement in his voice were equal to mine.

The critical time had passed and he was well enough to go home. I loaded him into the motor home and a happy and grateful Jeanette and Burt greeted me as soon as I pulled up. We returned Buzzie to his pen and to one other who seemed delighted to have him back: His feathered best friend and constant companion, a chicken.

The peacock at sixteen years old was still doing well. The operation itself was rare and when Buzzie dies another unusual happening will occur: Zoo personnel have agreed to do a post-mortem to see what the surgical sites look like and, perhaps, discover more information about gizzards.

Glenna and Richard Michaels owned five pairs of peacocks and hens for breeding purposes. Although the birds sometimes were kept in pens, more often they were allowed to roam the grounds, acting as watchdogs for the rambling Spanish-style house in Rancho Santa Fe. Giving the necessary shots or tests can be uneventful when compared to getting the birds in hand.

Glenna called to say one of the birds was sick and another was injured. Would I please come out and, while there, run any necessary routine tests on the others. I loaded the RV with supplies and drove on the eucalyptus-shaded and secluded road to their house.

I set up my make-shift examining area in the inner court yard while giving an occasional glance at my prospective patients. They were in every difficult to access area imaginable within the adobe brick walled courtyard —

on top of cars, on the roof of the house, barn and storage area, in the trees.

"All set," I called to their two employees who were going to help me.

"Right, Doc. We'll round 'em up. Joe, you get the ones on the ground, I'll go after the ones on the roofs."

No wild horse, goat or donkey roundup could have been more challenging nor laughable than the panorama of darting feathers and ear-piercing sounds that unfolded during the corralling. Although peacocks are not noted for speed or agility, these birds were crafty. Joe would walk cautiously behind a bird and the peacock or hen, sensing his presence, would move faster, cackling in annoyance. As he would take longer and quicker steps to keep up with the bird, the bird would increase its pace correspondingly and the cackle became a shriek.

Pete, on the roof, was having worse luck than Joe. As he approached a bird, it would let him get almost within reaching distance, then glide to the ground, shrieking all the way. Pete would climb down, follow the bird only to have it go back to the roof, making scolding, throaty noises.

The men soon discovered it took both of them working as a team to capture one bird. One man would head the bird towards the other who would lunge and grab the peacock. By the time the first bird finally was caught and brought to me, the captors were breathing heavily and perspiring profusely. Definitely, I had the easier job this day.

I charge extra for house calls because of the time, gasoline and overhead involved in simply getting to the residence. It is a good thing for the client that I set these fees by the number of pets treated or the medication or treatment required and not by the hour. By the time all the elusive peacocks and hens had been caught and treated, if I had charged an hourly fee plus testing and medication, the Michaels' bill would have looked almost as astronomical as the national debt!

6

Special Pets

If your pet was born with a handicap or has an accident or illness that requires surgery and leaves it "special," you will discover that with love and encouragement from you, the animal will respond and adapt well to its handicap. Like many of my clients who have handicapped pets, you will discover they make wonderful companions who are more affectionate than self-sufficient animals because of their dependency on you, the owner.

Of course, no one wants a normal pet to become handicapped so avoid obvious accidents. Never hit or kick a pet, watch out for the tails of dogs or cats when using a rocking chair or closing a door, look out for a kitten, puppy or rabbit who is apt to chew electrical cords and, do not let a bird out of its cage to roam because its inquisitiveness can lead it into trouble.

One floor-walking gray and yellow cockatiel explored its way inside a box, a roach trap, where it got stuck in the gooey poison meant for the insects. The bird was fortunate that the owners brought him to me immediately because if the poison remained on its feathers too long, it would have killed him. Although the thorough washing, cleaning and detoxification saved his life, he looked a bit peculiar afterwards: All his feathers came out. Eventually, the feathers grew back, the owner switched to a different roach exterminating product — and watched the cockatiel from then on whenever it was out of its cage.

Accidents happen even to pets of conscientious owners. The woman enjoyed the company of her umbrella cockatoo so much that she carried the white crested, eighteen-inch bird on her shoulder almost all the time, taking it everywhere she went in the house. One night, she started into the kitchen to check her bubbling vat of spaghetti on the stove, tripped and catapulted the bird on her shoulder into the pot. Quickly, disregarding any burns she might receive, she reached into the pot, grabbed the bird and immediately dried him. Even though the bird required intensive care, her quick thinking and actions saved him from an unpleasant death — and salvaged dinner that night, too.

An animal needs supervision and protection when moving to or visiting new surroundings, particularly if the pet is young and especially if the place is not at ground level. A dog or cat while chasing or playing can do serious harm to itself. In fact, so many cats living in sky scrapers fall from the balconies and windows that doctors have dubbed these often fatal accidents the "high rise syndrome." To protect a pet from this tragic ending, the animal should be tethered or a temporary or permanent wire enclosure constructed to keep it from going overboard.

A frantic owner of a two-year old black and tan Rottweiler called me because the dog fell from the second story of an apartment building. The woman was visiting a relative, the dog saw a butterfly as an enticing plaything to chase, jumped at it, shot over the railing and landed on the concrete below. The woman rushed him to me.

Amazingly, the x-rays showed that although he had fractures of both front legs, he had only minor internal injuries. An orthopedic surgeon operated and placed pins and bone screws in the joints and then a body splint. The animal spent two days recuperating in my clinic where we treated him for shock before he was released to his owner. He was fortunate that the injuries were not more extensive — or fatal.

 Risks to an animal are always present when it is allowed to roam freely outside. Dogs and cats are apt to get into fights, get hurt — or killed — by objects or cars, or eat dangerous or poisonous foods. Even animals that appear safe in cages outside can get into interesting predicaments like Jimmy, the gray cockatiel.

"I think you should come out as soon as possible, Doctor," Louise said over the phone. "I don't know what's wrong but one of our birds is looking funny."

"How is it looking funny?" I asked, hoping for more information before I left for her home.

"I can't explain it. He just looks — weird. I think you should take a look."

"All right," I agreed. "I'll be there in about two hours."

I packed the medical kit with supplies for the most common accidents and as I drove to the house, wondered what might have happened. My conclusion: Be prepared to find almost anything.

Louise led me through the house to the bird's cage located outside on a cement patio, about eight feet from a canyon area covered with thick underbrush. The five- by two- by four-foot cage had bars spaced about one inch apart. I glanced at the birds and Louise was right, one of them looked strange — lopsided would perhaps best describe it.

"Last night," she said, "I heard noises, got out of bed and looked out the window. I didn't see anything but this morning when I came out to feed them, I noticed Jimmy looked funny. That's when I called you."

As she talked, I walked around the cage, looking for anything out of the ordinary. I saw no blood but — I stooped over and picked up — one-half of a cockatiel wing!

"I know what at least a part of the problem is." I showed her what I found. "Let me look at Jimmy." I opened the cage and the bird let me catch him without a struggle.

Good grief! Small wonder he looked peculiar. One wing was completely missing and the other one was gone from the elbow down. Obviously, the noise she heard last night was the scuffle between a wild animal from the canyon, tempted by a trapped, plump dinner, when it reached through the cage and grabbed the unwilling meal by its wings. But what kind of animal? A member of the rodent family would not have the grasping capabilities needed. Possums are usually not that aggressive. A person — maybe, but what would be the motive? A raccoon — possibly.

"Looks like an animal, probably a raccoon, attacked Jimmy." I rolled the bird from side to side in my hands, examining the area, astonished that I still could not see any blood around the wounds. "These exposed areas need to be closed and treated to prevent infection. I'll have to take him to the clinic to do it."

A thorough examination of Jimmy at the clinic showed that the remaining part of the wing would have to be removed because it was mutilated and damaged beyond repair. I called Louise, explained the extent of his wounds, the costs to do the surgery, informed her that he would require extensive care during his recovery and, of course, would never fly again.

She was quiet, reflecting on the news for a while. "Why don't you put him to sleep? I mean, a bird with no wings! Not much of a life for him — and a lot of extra work for me."

"He could be a companion for the other bird and a nice pet."

"No. I don't want him," she said without hesitation. "Put him to sleep."

Euthanizing a pet is a dreaded task and not one I do unless absolutely necessary. In Jimmy's case, I thought he could tolerate the loss of both wings and still be a delightful pet for someone.

"If you don't want Jimmy," I replied, "why don't you sign him over to me? Perhaps I can find a home for him when he's well enough to leave here."

"Sounds fine to me," she replied. I thought I heard a sigh of relief.

Within a few hours after Jimmy's surgery, he began eating, chirping, hopping around and climbing the sides of the cage. The speedy recuperative and adaptive powers of birds have never ceased to amaze me.

I received a phone call from Louise a few days later. She had heard another ruckus from the bird area the night before, dashed out and frightened away the culprit, a fox.

"Well, well," I commented. "I didn't think we had foxes in the area. To safeguard your other bird, you should get a cage with smaller openings or put a fine mesh wire around the cage so the fox can't reach in or move the bird into the safety of the house."

"Yes, I will make some changes," she replied. "How's Jimmy doing? Have you found a home for him?"

"Jimmy's doing just fine," I replied with pleasure, "and he has a new home. A couple who recently lost a handicapped bird, who had a most rewarding experience with it, were absolutely thrilled to have Jimmy."

Although this owner was thoughtful about her bird in many respects, she overlooked a danger that proved to be extremely harmful to Petey. And, as far as what I think about birds who are allowed to free-fly in the house, Petey is an example of what can and does happen, all too often.

"Help, Doctor Ewing!" the woman's voice blurted out the instant I said hello. "I don't know what's wrong. His feet are all swollen and he's having real trouble perching."

"Whoa. Slow down. First of all, who is this?"

"I'm sorry. This is Virginia Newsome, you know Petey's mother — Petey, the parakeet."

She'd slowed her speech a bit but it was obvious she was upset. Mrs. Newsome, yes, I remembered her well. A conscientious pet owner who frequently became overly distraught when one of her pets was ill.

"I don't know exactly what's the matter but he can't bend his toes."

"Would you like me to take a look at Petey?"

"Oh, yes, and as soon as possible."

I thumbed through my appointment book. "I can be out there in about an hour. Now, don't worry. I'm sure I can fix Petey up in no time."

"Thanks," she said, "I'm so grateful you can come soon. I just don't know what to make of it. I'm so worried."

"See you shortly. Relax, Petey's going to be all right — really."

Within the hour, I rapped on the front door. Virginia opened it before I had even finished knocking.

"I'm so glad your here. Come this way."

We sprinted to the dining room where the blue parakeet was housed. I removed him from the cage and immediately examined his feet. Assuredly, he had a problem. Each toe and foot had many punctures in it and each was badly infected.

"Does Petey still fly around the house?" I arched an eyebrow and looked at her sternly because during the last house call, I had recommended to her as I do to other pet owners that for safety reasons, a bird should not be allowed to free-fly: Its curiosity often leads to harmful and dangerous areas and situations.

Like a child scolded by a parent, she nodded her head and glanced down at the floor remorsefully. Under her breath she mumbled, "But he likes to fly about."

Something sharp had caused Petey's problem. "Show me where his favorite places to roost are. We need to find whatever did this to his feet."

As she pointed out his landing places, I checked them. From the high curtain rods in the dining room to the low kitchen cupboards, I ran my hand over each surface but did not find anything sharp or abrasive.

I looked quizzically at his cage. "You don't suppose it could be — "

I walked over to it, ran my hand around the inside of it and then over the entry to the cage. "Ouch!" I found the source of the problem.

When the door area had been cut, the wires had not been smoothed or filed and needle-like ends were left, protruding upward into the cage entry. No wonder he had multiple wounds: Each time he flew back to the cage, he had to land on these points and would puncture his feet.

"Here's the problem." I showed her. "You're going to have to get another cage or devise some way to cover those pointed edges. As for Petey, he has a severe bacterial infection that these medications should cure. However, his feet are badly damaged," and, I thought to myself, I'm not sure if he'll ever be able to bend his toes but at this point, there was no need to worry her more. "Let me know how he responds to the treatment and the condition of his toes after a few days."

Virginia called two days later informing me that the drugs took care of the infection but, as I anticipated, he still could not bend his toes. "I've covered the area and made a landing pad as you suggested," she continued, sounding pleased, "sort of a front porch to his cage that covers the wires and is quite smooth. He won't get cut again."

She called back a few weeks later with a glowing condition and progress report. "I've made ramps for him also as you mentioned so he can easily walk to some of his favorite places and flat perches in other areas. And, he's learned how to balance without being able to grab with his feet. His flat feet don't seem to keep him from doing what he wants to."

Petey was fortunate. Few birds cope well with this kind of handicap but, because of the constant attention of this attentive owner, he had adjusted to his handicap.

During the next four years, I got to see the creative additions she continued to make for Petey whenever she would call me out to reexamine him or care for other family pets. Petey was doing fine until the next year when Virginia called me with sad news. A week before, she had left the front door open and Petey flew away. She searched door-to-door, put announcements on telephone poles and advertised in newspapers.

"Is there — anything else — I can do?" she choked out, alternating between crying and blowing her nose.

Although I would have liked to have reminded her about my warning regarding free-flying birds, this was an inappropriate time for a "I told you so" lecture. Petey was gone and she undoubtedly was punishing herself enough for his escape. Now, she, not the bird, was the one who desperately needed help.

"I can't think of anything you haven't done regarding Petey, however, you sound so depressed. Why don't you call one of the animal support groups such as The Delta Society?

"I — I didn't know such groups existed." She blew her nose again and snuffed. "Please, tell me about them."

"These organizations have trained volunteers to help people get through the devastating time after a pet dies or disappears. Most of them are nonprofit, rely on donations to help support them and offer free counseling. I'm sure if you call, one of the staff can help you through this crisis."

It was a Friday before a three day holiday weekend — the beginning of the time when most veterinarians and physicians agree that, if an emergency is going to happen, it will. This day was no exception.

The panicky man bolted into the clinic with the limp body of a five-week-old kitten in his hands. A quick check of the kitten's eyes, the mucous membrane of the inner lips and its ears showed it was in shock and anemic from loss of blood.

"Begin a transfusion immediately," I said to my assistant. "I'll be there in a moment." Pam, seeing the seriousness of the condition and understanding the urgency in my voice, moved instantly, taking the nearly lifeless kitten with her.

"What happened?" I asked the owner.

Haltingly, he told his sad story. He was leaving his home to go shopping, walked around the front of his car, got in, started the engine and backed out. He neglected to check behind the car and ran over the sleeping kitten.

"Can you do something?" he muttered, shaking his head in disbelief and rubbing the frown lines that criss-crossed his forehead. "I'm so sorry. I don't believe I did it! Please, please help him."

"We'll do the best we can and I can guess how you must feel. By bringing in the kitten immediately, you have done the best for him. I need to check him and must take x-rays to find out the extent of the injuries. While I'm doing that," I handed him a paper, "fill out this information form and by the time you finish, I should be able to tell you more."

I left the room, reflecting on the tragedy of this accident as I walked towards the emergency room. Having a kitten or any baby animal is the same as having the responsibility of a toddler. An alert, caring parent would not consider backing out a car without checking behind it for a small child — neither should a pet owner.

By the time I got to the kitten, he was responding to the transfusion and managed to partially open his eyes when I gently touched him. What an unusual color they were; instead of being yellow, his were golden. And his fur was a color different than most orange tabbies; it was a warm, mustard color. The white fluffy tuft of hair under his chin quivered as he weakly opened his mouth trying to meow.

"Poor little fellow," I lamented, gently finger-stroking his head. "I'm going to try my best to save you."

I lowered the x-ray machine, adjusted it to the proper height and took the necessary exposures while talking comfortingly to him. "I'll be back in a few minutes. You're gonna be fine," I said aloud — and hoped I was right.

The developed x-rays showed he had oblique fractures of both femurs, a pelvic fracture and a rupture of the abdomen, not through the skin, but through the abdominal lining. I consulted with my assistants and because the kitten had reacted well to the transfusion, we agreed that the bones could be set, however, because of the extent of the injuries, someone with expertise in setting complicated bone fractures should be called in.

I walked back into the waiting room where the owner was pacing the perimeter of the room. Indeed, he seemed quite concerned about his pet.

"We've stabilized the kitten's condition but he is badly hurt and I recommend a specialist, an orthopedic surgeon, to do the surgery. I called one and he's available tomorrow. Although his fees will be about 800 dollars, I think his skills are necessary."

"I don't care what it costs," he said. "I want the best for my kitten."

"I'm glad you are willing to see he gets good care — he's a beautiful little fellow. I will need a down payment of 400 dollars before we can begin."

"Of course, no problem," he replied. "My check-book is in the car. I'll get it and be right back." He turned and almost ran from the room.

"Good," I shouted, smiling at the positive reaction this owner had.

In the distance, I heard the sound of a car starting. I waited a few minutes and when he did not return, opened the door and looked into the parking lot. It was empty. The man had left.

Now I had another problem: Although the owner had filled in the basic information form, he had not signed the paper that gave permission to perform the required surgery. Because of the legalities involved, I could not do anything without this signed consent form. During the next few days, my staff and I took turns calling the phone numbers he had given. We left message after message at home and at his work place. He did not return our calls.

The kitten lay in the kennel until Tuesday, the first working day that we could possibly do anything because most of the staff was off, enjoying the holiday weekend. When all returned to work, I called them together to discuss our options. One, we could euthanize him and end his suffering, or, because it seemed obvious the pet was abandoned, we could operate at our own expense and on our own time, without the aid of a specialist. Although we might not be able to set his bones and suture his wound as well as an orthopedic surgeon, we could try. The staff decision was rapid and unanimous: Surgery was scheduled for the next day.

Once anesthetized, my surgical assistant and I put pins in both legs and wrapped wire around the bones to hold them to the pins. These pins and wires would be a permanent part of each leg and, in time, the bone would grow around them. As the pinning and wiring proceeded, the pelvis came into alignment by itself. Next was the abdominal rupture and, by far, the most taxing part of the surgery because trying to suture it was as difficult as sewing a rubber sheet with a dull needle.

We finished in about three hours, the patient was doing well and, if this golden creature was to be our guest for a while, he needed a name. Heads were scratched, thinking caps put on and the resulting name approved by all. Similar to the unforgettable character in Dickens' *A Christmas Carol*, our little fellow with a leg problem would be called, not Tiny Tim, but simply Timmie.

Within twenty-four hours, Timmie was trying to stand but with difficulty. Because of the bandages, surgery and some damage to the nerves affecting the lower part of his right leg, he was not able to move properly and his leg would buckle at the ankle. To help him stand, we added a splint on that side.

As the days passed and he became more active, Timmie needed an area larger than the cage to move about in so, four days after surgery, I took him home, much to the chagrin of my tortoiseshell cat, Scamper, who had to take a rear seat to Timmie's needs. Within two to three weeks, Timmie was running, jumping and attacking my dethroned and offended cat.

Two months after surgery, I took him back to the clinic for declawing and x-rays. The developed x-rays showed good news: His legs were healing even better than I thought they would.

Two years later, the unobservant person would not know anything had ever occurred to him. To the truly observant, however, he has a slight bow in the right leg and a sway to his backbone — possibly from surgery when we put tension on the muscles on the right side of the body that attach to the backbone. And, when sitting, he has an unusual posture because sometimes he tends to kick the right leg to the side.

I do not think he's aware of it but, he is handicapped to a certain degree. However, if my staff and I had not decided to try the surgery, I would not have the pleasure of one of the most affectionate cats I have known — and a cat who purrs with such vigor it is almost ear-shattering.

Many compassionate people cannot resist buying or accepting an animal with a handicap because they feel sorry for them and believe they can help. The rewards these people receive by adopting a handicapped pet are many. Because the animal is more dependent on the owner, they are most affectionate. In my opinion, handicapped animals make the best pets.

Even if the handicapped pet appears healthy, the first place the owners should take a new pet is to the veterinarian for a checkup and a professional evaluation of the animal's handicap. In many cases, the veterinarian can offer advice about how best to care for the animal or suggest ways to help it better adjust to its disability.

In this instance, Martha brought in Rocky, a six-inch land turtle she had purchased that morning, not for a routine examination but because he had an infection. It was apparent to her that the pet store was not giving him the proper care.

"There he was," she said with an obvious British accent, "looking up at me so pathetically with his one good eye, all infected. And, where the other eye used to be — ugh. It was a mess of draining liquid. How could I resist him? He needed me."

Examining a turtle is not too difficult — once he stretches his head and legs out of his shell, that is. However, getting him to come out of this protective hideout when you want him to is another story. One can have patience and bide time until he decides to emerge, tempt him with food and hope he is hungry enough to stick his head out or tickle him.

With Rocky, repeated tickles to a back foot encouraged him to stick his head out far enough for me to grab his neck. I cleaned his eye areas with a topical medication, disinfected them and injected a systemic antibiotic in his leg in an area equivalent to a human's armpit.

In a week, his sighted eye had healed and the orbit of the other was filling in. He ate well, gobbling down his meals of fresh vegetables and a blended combination of dog and cat food with an added vitamin and mineral supplement. Because he needed to be examined often during the time he was in the clinic, he got so used to being tickled then petted that he appeared to enjoy it, turning his head to the side or lifting it up so a scratching finger could reach the area he wanted rubbed. In fact, as turtles go, one could say Rocky became quite affectionate.

She was an orange tabby about six months old and a wild canyon cat who a concerned neighborhood resident saw, managed to catch and bring to me because its left eye was badly infected and swollen shut. The woman was not the owner nor could she keep the cat nor would she pay for any treatments but she felt sorry for the cat and hoped I could do something for it.

As soon as possible, I tranquilized the cat, then examined the eye to find that, unfortunately, the eyeball was permanently damaged and required removal. After scraping and cleaning the whole orbit, I placed a surgical sponge in it to give form to the eye area before sewing the eyelid shut.

She was running about in a few days, had her worming medicine, all necessary vaccinations and now only lacked a home. My staff and I began mentioning our newest addition to clients in the hopes that someone would want her.

The tabby was with us for about two weeks when a woman and her daughter, volunteers for Mercy Crusade, came to the clinic to bring me a seriously ill dog for treatment. All it took was a quick glance at the cat by the daughter and an instant love affair blossomed.

"What a precious darling. Poor dear, only one eye." She reached her fingers through the cage and stroked the cat under the chin. The cat purred with happiness. "What happened to her? Such a sweetheart," she cooed.

I barely had finished with the explanation of tabby's operation and homeless background and she had the cage open, scooped up the cat and snuggled the furry ball close in her arms.

"Look no farther, Doc! I'll take her," she said. "She's — just precious. That's it! Precious — that's what I'll name her. No more the outside life of hunger, getting into trouble or fights. You now have a house to live in." The cat closed its eye, lifted its head a bit higher as the young woman gently scratched her under the chin and, as if replying to her new owner, sighed in obvious contentment.

Ginn, a blue and white parakeet, had splayed legs, a condition where the legs do not grow properly because of inadequate nutrition while in the egg or during the first few days of hatching or, sometimes, due to a genetic inheritance. If this crippling occurrence is discovered soon after hatching, it usually can be corrected by putting the bird in a lower body cast to hold the legs in the correct growing position. Ginn's problem was not diagnosed early enough and he was permanently handicapped. The owners purchased the bird even with his disability because they wanted him to have a good home and were willing to work with him.

Like other birds with this problem, he was not able to grasp easily with his feet, only with his beak, so he frequently was picked up and moved about by the owner. Because of this, Ginn was held more often than a bird without a handicap and the bond between owner and pet flourished.

Another bird, Monty, was a typical attractive half-moon conure: He was green with colorful accent areas of orange and blue. Unfortunately, he had abnormal, crippled feet that are usually caused by a nutritional deficiency, genetic defect, or an infectious organism. The owners brought him to me because they thought that even with his deformity, he did not have as good a balance or was not able to move about as well as he used to. Although the radiological study and x-rays I took showed nothing out of the ordinary, I decided to have them reviewed by Doctor Silverman, a San Francisco radiologist, hoping that he might find something I did not.

Doctor Silverman called me to say this was, as I suspected, an extremely unusual case. After careful study, he was sure that because of his crippled feet and inability to move about easily, he had fallen and fractured his spine sometime in the past. This injury, compounded with his crippled feet, was the reason he was not moving better.

Now that the doctor had pinpointed the cause, I could suggest the best way to treat the problem. I called the owners, relayed the information that Doctor Silverman discovered and recommended they feed Monty a nutritionally well-balanced diet, handle him carefully to prevent any further falls, place all perches at low levels and, in case he might fall again, put padding in the bottom of the cage. Again, as in other cases where the owners showered a pet with concern and love, Monty became a more affectionate and friendly companion than he had been.

Deaf animals are especially dependent upon owners because they cannot hear an approaching car, an enemy or a call to "come here." Communicating with them can only be done by hand signals when one stands directly in front of the animal and when it is looking at the person. For their safety, these animals should be kept on a leash when outside.

Some animals are particularly susceptible to deafness, such as white long-haired cats with blue eyes. But I had not expected one with yellow eyes to have inherited this genetic defect.

My wife found her abandoned in the apartment building we lived in and named her Mai Khao, Thai for white silk because of her gossamer coat. I did not realize she was deaf until about two weeks after we adopted her and came home one evening announcing our arrival with slamming doors and loud voices. I walked into the living room and found her curled up in a ball, sleeping soundly. I reached down, touched her, and she nearly jumped out of her skin! She had not heard us come home.

Mai Khao, like most handicapped animals, was anxious to please and learned to obey hand signals quickly. She also was most loving and delighted in being petted and touched. Perhaps, because she could not hear when I praised or talked affectionately to her, she needed to be caressed more than a hearing animal.

Sometimes a disease, lifesaving surgery or an accident of unknown origin causes a pet's handicap. When this occurs, the owner plays an important part in how well an animal responds to the affliction. If a close relationship develops between the pet and owner, the recuperative power of the animal is helped dramatically.

My clients have told me and I have observed how well an animal can adapt to an amputation or a handicap, but until I was given a three- to five-year-old bright blue parakeet, blind in both eyes to observe, I did not realize how quickly a sightless bird could adjust. I do not know whether this bird was born blind or if the blindness resulted from a trauma or a nutritional deficiency early in life. However, unless told, one would never know she could not see because she moved around the cage without hesitation, playing with toys and going unerringly to food and water when necessary.

How long would it take for her to adapt to new surroundings and how would she do it? I removed the parakeet from its familiar square cage and placed her in an unfamiliar rectangular one, on the center of the perch so she could not touch any part of the cage. At first, the bird sat still without making so much as a subtle chirp. Then, just as we use our hands to explore unknown surroundings, she used her beak to reach up, arching her head and "feeling" in a semicircle in the space above, next to probe the area in front and below her until she hung upside down on the perch. She grabbed the perch with her beak and righted herself. Then, one careful step to the right and, again, the same searching pattern until she touched the side of the cage.

She grasped the bars of the cage with her feet and cautiously moved to the end of that side, went along the next side, then to the far end where the food and water bowls were located. After a brief time out for drinking and eating, she continued along the bars until she reached her starting point. She then started to the top of the cage using the wires like a step ladder. After a thorough exploration of this area, she worked her way to the bottom of the enclosure where she walked around the entire papered tray. Each of her search patterns was methodical and thorough and, in about an hour, she moved about the cage as well as any sighted bird.

The owners of Thumper, a brown and white rabbit, brought him to me because he was holding his head tilted to the right side and when he hopped, he would fall and roll over and had difficulty standing. After an examination, I concluded that his affliction had not been caused by a trauma or blow to the head but, most likely from an ear infection or mites that effect the inner ear and balance mechanism.

I delivered the sad news to the owners that the chances of totally correcting this problem were negligible at this time but, this was a disability Thumper could adjust to and they could help him do it. I suggested massaging the head area as often as possible and holding him upright until he learned how to rebalance himself.

With the helpful, encouraging attitude of the owners, within two weeks he had regained his balance, in three weeks he was moving about by himself and, according to the owners, his head tilt was less severe than it was when they first brought him to me.

"And, Doctor Ewing," she said, "I don't know if it's because we've paid so much attention to him during the past few weeks or patted and praised him so often, but whatever — he is a much better, more attentive pet than he was."

Animals adapt well to handicaps, even those handicaps that might seem insurmountable. The owners of a tan Afghan hound brought the handsome dog in because it had leg problems. The x-rays showed masses in the right front and left rear leg that the referring veterinarian felt certain were malignant bone tumors. Because he would have to amputate both legs, he recommended euthanizing the animal. The owners loved their pet deeply and decided that even after amputation, if they had to lift and carry him about and give him physical therapy for the rest of his life, these chores would be worth it just to have the pleasure of his company. They adamantly refused the thought of euthanizing him and directed us to operate.

A few months after surgery and chemical therapy, the owners had an unexpected and pleasant surprise. Because of their caring and encouragement, the dog learned to stand by itself, to balance and even to move about in a hopping fashion!

Roger, a four year old, forty-five pound gray shepherd mix, was an exceptional dog in many ways. He was even tempered, affectionate, always eager to please his owner and Roberta Morgan's most cherished pet. After the illness was diagnosed and an operation performed, his courage and adaptability made him even more exceptional.

The first doctor Roberta took Roger to, shook his head and defined Roger's paralysis of the hind limbs as spinal cancer and referred her to a specialist. This doctor, a board certified surgeon, operated but was unable to remove all the cancer. He suggested that if the paralysis persisted, Roger should be euthanized.

Roberta simply would not accept this and told the doctor she was going to take Roger home and care for him. He informed her that to properly care for him at home, the advice of a veterinarian who would come to the house would be necessary. He referred her to me.

When I first saw Roger, he was bandaged from the surgery and lying on a blanket in the family room. I reached down, scratching him behind the ear and he licked my hand and looked at me with large, brown eyes. I felt certain that if he could have, he would have wagged his tail.

"Outside of love and affection, until his surgery heals and the bandages are off, there is not much you can do in the physical therapy line. Then, you need to move, stretch and massage his legs several times a day in the hopes of getting some feeling back in them. For the most benefit to Roger, these exercises should be done in water."

I glanced at her petite size and wondered if she had the strength necessary not only to lift Roger up and over the side of a bathtub but, to do it without hurting herself. I decided it was too much for her to tackle by herself.

"Why don't you get an inflatable child's swimming pool, fill it with warm water, put him in it and exercise his legs there. It will be much easier for you to lift him over its low sides than the high ones of a bathtub."

Roberta thought the pool was a good idea and the treatment schedule could be easily accomplished. She would exercise his legs in the morning before work, come home during the lunch hour and give another treatment and then another after work.

"I'm so glad I called you, Doctor Ewing. I was about to think any doctor I talked to would label him hopeless and suggest putting him to sleep. I just can't bear to do that — at least not now. He is still so loving and doesn't seem to be in pain. Of course, if he was suffering, I would have to — " The next word stuck in her throat. She cleared her voice and dabbed a tissue to her eyes before continuing. "But I have time to work with him and as long as he seems happy, I want to try everything, anything, to help him."

"There is something I saw advertised in one of my veterinary journals that you might want to consider for Roger. It might just be the ticket for him."

"What is that?" she asked, a spark of excitement crept into her voice.

"Let's see if I can describe it. It's a stretcher-like device, a dolly of sorts, with holes in it so the rear legs can dangle through and has two wheels so the dog can pull itself along with its front legs. If Roger will use it, he could get exercise and be mobile."

"It does sound appropriate for him! He could go outside and he loves the outdoors so." She bent over patting his head and smiling at him. "You'd like to go out, wouldn't you, Roger?" Roger responded with juicy licks to her hand.

"Could you call me with the information about how to order it?"

"Of course." I grinned, extremely pleased with her willingness to work with Roger and the degree to which she volunteered to help him.

Roger's surgery healed in about three weeks and Roberta began his water treatments. Although she worked with him diligently through the following months, the feeling in his hind quarters did not return. He was permanently paralyzed.

I got a phone call from Roberta, asking if I could come to her house because Roger's walker, as she referred to it, had arrived and she was not sure how to put him in it. I scheduled time during the next day.

She had the unit assembled, placed outside, and ready to put Roger in it by the time I arrived. With her help, I put it under him, placed his hind legs in the holes and, apparently sensing what this apparatus was for, he took a hesitant step forward with one front paw.

"Roger! Good boy! Come here, fella. Come here."

True to his obedient nature, Roger cautiously moved towards her. "That's wonderful." She rewarded him with a hug around his neck and a kiss on his forehead.

Like a child with a new scooter, Roger began learning what he could do — and not do — with his new "wheels." He started forward with more assurance this time. Perhaps with a bit too much confidence because he hit a bump and tipped over.

"Poor boy. That's okay," she consoled him as we righted him. "Accidents will happen."

Roger, on the other hand, did not seem the least concerned over his upset. He darted forward eagerly, panting with excitement.

As time passed, Roger learned how to help Roberta get him in the device by putting himself in the best position for her to lift him. According to her, he loved being outside and, because the house was on a cul-de-sac and she could walk with him and not worry about traffic, they spent a great deal of time in the fresh air and his physique showed it; his front legs and shoulders bulged with muscles.

One day, I got a phone call from Roberta, needing my advice. Roger had found his favorite ball in the yard that they used to play catch with. Did I suppose it would be okay for her to throw the ball for him?

"I think so. Try it."

"I'm afraid he'll hurt himself. I don't think I should." She sounded so concerned, skeptical and even frightened that I could not help but offer to assist.

"I doubt that he'll have a problem but, would you like me to come out? I haven't seen Roger in a while anyway."

"Oh, yes. That would be wonderful!"

Roger was in his walker, in the front of the house when I pulled up. I got out of the car and walked over to him. "Hi! How're you doing, Roger? Want to play?"

He cocked his head to one side and looked at me questioningly then over towards Roberta who was holding the ball. "Woof!" He shifted his weight anxiously from front paw to front paw.

"Go ahead, throw it," I said to her.

She threw the ball and off he galloped, picking it up and returning it to her to throw it again. The retrieving game continued for several more throws until, unfortunately, the ball bounced over the curb and stopped in the grass beyond. Roger, full speed ahead hit the curb, was thrown off balance and fell over into the grass.

We dashed over and quickly set him upright on the asphalt. "Woof," he barked looking at the ball longingly and panting. "Woof, woof," he barked still staring at his toy.

"Throw it again," I suggested, "but try to keep it in the street."

Roberta threw and Roger chased, returning it to her time after time. Then she heaved it too hard and it ricocheted over the curb again.

"Oh, no!" She started towards the ball to get it before the dog would upset in his haste to retrieve it.

"Wait a minute," I said. "Let's see what he does this time."

Roger sped towards the ball but when he got to the curb he stopped. Slowly and carefully, he pulled his walker, one wheel at a time, over the curb onto the grass and picked up the ball. It was obvious his favorite game was not going to be stopped by something as minor as a curb.

Because of the affection, concern and determined attitude of Roberta to keep Roger alive as long as possible, he lived two more years. Had she decided to euthanize him when suggested, he would have missed those years filled with enjoyment and she would have been denied the companionship and enhancement to her life that he gave. He was given not only more time to be loved but to give love in return.

Pets and Their People

A veterinarian, or any doctor for that matter, treats not only the patient but must deal with the "family," which in my case are the owners of the animal or animals. Occasionally, these people or where they lived or their engrossing conversations were more fascinating than their pets.

One such case was a professor of comparative re-
ligions at a local university and his wife. At first, Tom
called me out to care for their black cat Bunny who was
allowed to roam outdoors and was extremely accident
prone. I was at their house at least once every three months
to repair Bunny's cuts from a fence, or find out why he was
limping or had a runny nose, or to treat scratches, or a torn
toenail — and the list goes on. Because of seeing the cat
and visiting the owners so often, we eventually began
discussing topics other than the cat's maladies. Tom liked
to philosophize and discuss current events and I delighted
in listening and sharing my views, too.

As Bunny got older, he settled down and spent more
time indoors and his accidents became fewer. Still Tom
would ask me over quarterly to check out Bunny and chat
for a while. I would look forward to our get-togethers and
schedule my house call appointment with at least an extra
half hour for socializing.

Sometimes the person and the surroundings were
both unique and in the case of this elderly woman in eastern
San Diego, both qualifications were easily met. I would
arrive at her house at the specified time and she would be

waiting for me behind a seven-foot-high chain link fence — waiting to unlock the three chains with three padlocks that secured the gate. The area inside the fence was an absolute disaster. There was a car half covered with dirt, shopping carts, oil drums, wooden cartons, piles of lumber, posts, fencing material, empty glass bottles, rusting cans and other kinds of unidentifiable trash. Palm fronds had littered the ground and stayed undisturbed for so long that birds were nesting in them.

I followed the scraggly-haired, scarecrow-like woman down the narrow debris-covered path towards the house, stepping over or moving things out of the way as I went. About one-third of the way down the path I stopped because I had learned from previous visits that I would not be asked inside — she never asked me inside — and here was as suitable an area as any in the yard to set up my outdoor clinic. I cleaned off the top of an oil drum for my work table and off-loaded the top of stacked-up, hardened cement bags as a place to set my equipment. I glanced around. This was like working in a junk yard in the jungle and reminded me of my duty in Southeast Asia!

By the time I was through organizing, she was walking from the house carrying or coaxing an animal towards me. I examined or did what was necessary to the dog or cat and she would then return it to the house and bring out another. This process continued until all the animals she thought needed attention were treated.

During the examination or treatment of the pet, interspersed with talk about the condition or care of the animal, she would tell me how neighbors threw things over the fence or how they were trying to break in and steal her pets. Obviously, she was paranoid and perhaps senile. In addition to her mental problems, she had limited funds and if it had not been for the help of Mercy Crusade, her pets would have gone without adequate medical attention.

Her cats had fewer problems than her dogs who had skin dermatitis from flea allergies and an occasional intestinal problem, undoubtedly due to something they ate that was crawling, vegetating or decomposing in the yard. Because she always brought each pet outside, I knew how many animals I treated that day but I had no idea exactly how many animals she actually kept inside. I think probably six or seven dogs and at least six cats. I also have no idea how the inside of her house looked but I certainly think I can make a well-founded guess.

Kat, a lanky gray tabby, had a case history that was not too unusual for a stray canyon cat. What was a bit out of the ordinary was making a house call there one day.

Kat would come up to Mary's and her father Bill's house twice a day to be fed, then return to his hideout somewhere in the ravine behind the house. As far as medical treatment, I could provide Mary and Bill with powders that could be easily added to his food for internal parasites but to vaccinate him was another story. When it was time for his inoculations, they could successfully coax him into their small bathroom before I arrived but, once there, my task of trying to hold him with one hand while leaning around the toilet and injecting him with the other was always challenging.

When Kat was about ten years old, Bill called me out because "Kat is moping around and doesn't look good." When I arrived, the cat was lying stretched out and motionless. I reached down and easily picked him up with not so much as a threatening hiss. Indeed, their was something wrong with this feisty feline pugilist.

I took him to the clinic for tests and the results showed he had a viral infection and feline infectious peritonitis, FIP. For his own well being, Kat must become a house dweller.

After his one week stay in the hospital, he got used to confinement and although the owners were not sure he would settle down in their house, they agreed to try to keep him indoors and also to try to get the oral medicines down him themselves. At the end of three weeks, they were able to pet him: Kat had reconciled himself to the comforts of indoor living.

As I mentioned, there was a unique aspect to this case that did not deal with the pet. During the three previous house calls after I treated Kat, Bill, who followed the stock market closely, and I would sit down and discuss the market. He was a knowledgeable, personable man, I guessed in his mid- to late fifties, about six-foot tall and with a slender build. One time he was dressed in a business suit, another time jeans and a work shirt and another, casual sport clothes. Although I credit myself with an open mind and the ability to accept other lifestyles, I still found myself stifling a gasp when Bill opened the door on this day.

He was dressed to the nines: high heels, hose, a skirt and blouse, eye makeup, rouge, lipstick and a shoulder length brown wig. I tried not to show surprise but I am sure my eyes widened and my mouth dropped open. I truly did not know what to say — which is a rarity for me — so decided the best response to his attire was to pretend he looked no different than usual. After I treated Kat, we sat down and discussed the market as if it were a house call like any other one. To this day, I will never know why he chose to dress up for me because in the numerous house calls that followed, nothing was ever said about that afternoon and he never again wore women's clothes when I was present.

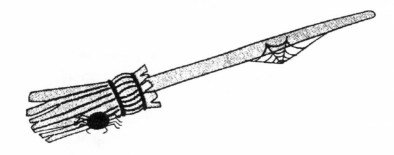

Peg, a slender woman in her thirties, had twelve cats of varying sizes, colors and sexes that, for the most part, had the usual flea skin problems and viral cat diseases. When one or the other was ill, she would bring it to the clinic or ask me to come to her house but, only after she had consulted with her friends.

"Doctor Ewing, I think you need to come immediately. Mary told me that Betsy, you know, my spotted cat is not feeling well. It seems that she has a stomach ache and you know Mary is one of the best when it comes to the laying on of hands. So I believe — "

"Whoa, Peg," I interrupted. "I know how much you believe in Mary's diagnoses, however, I need a few more facts." One of the hardest problems I always had with Peg was to have an opportunity to ask a few questions. It was as though once she started talking, she had no off switch. "Let's start with the cat's symptoms."

This situation was no different than my usual call from Peg. Not only did her friends diagnose problems by the laying on of hands but they used psychic readings, ouija boards, seances or other ways of foretelling the future to analyze her animals and let her know where they were hurting or what the problem was.

In one instance, one of her friends with the help of an ouija board, informed Peg that Missy the cat had a urinary problem. She was right, too. I ran tests on the animal and found she had feline urological syndrome, FUS, common among cats and thought to be diet related. Although the psychics were not always right, interestingly enough, they were right about fifty percent of the time.

Peg brought one of her cats, Blackbeard, into the clinic for me to examine because he had developed a growth on the side of his face, under the skin. Although not rare, this cutaneous horn as it is called is not all that common either. The growth is composed of material similar to an animal's horn and generally is a finger-shaped projection but in his case, when I felt it, it had more of a flattened mushroom shape.

There was only one thing to do. The growth needed to be removed surgically — to be excised — no, not to be exorcised!

Not all my cases were "hands on" situations with animals. Because of my travels in the military and being well-known in the avian field, I would often get phone calls wanting advice about how to care for sick pets from military personnel whose pets I had treated before they relocated or persons who had been referred to me by other veterinarians. Diagnosis by a long distance phone call was not unusual.

The owners of a parakeet breeding ranch in Oklahoma got my name from a reference in a pet bird magazine.

They contacted their local veterinarian who knew me from seminars I had given and he suggested that they call me.

There was obvious concern in Bob's voice as we talked and, as a bird breeder, he had reason to worry. Many of his birds were dying and the local veterinarian did not know why. He wondered if there was anything I could do to help them solve this serious situation.

In order to come up with any kind of diagnosis, I needed to examine a bird. Because of the distance involved and the fact that birds are not easily or safely transported, it would not be feasible to send me a live parakeet so I suggested that when one died, to preserve it and send it to me so I could get a pathological work-up done and then a diagnosis.

I should have given them more details about how to ship the bird carcass properly because the first sample they sent was not appropriate: The bird was frozen. I suspected we might be dealing with a viral condition but nothing could be confirmed with this specimen because body cells burst when frozen making it impossible for the pathologist to do a proper diagnostic post-mortem.

I called and asked them to send another bird and to keep it extremely cold, not frozen, by placing frozen ice packs around it, wrapping it with insulation such as newspaper and then sending it by overnight express mail. They followed my directions, the post-mortem was done and I could diagnose the problem. Unfortunately, the results were not good.

The birds had polyomavirus, a genus of the papovavirus, that is highly infectious and transmitted by the adult bird through its feather dust and excrement and results in up to a one hundred percent mortality rate in hatchlings less than fifteen days old. The prescribed treatment is identical to hoof-and-mouth disease in large animals — eradication of all animals and introducing new breeding stock.

The owners, after hearing this devastating news, did not want to kill the entire flock. "Isn't there anything else we can do?"

"Well," I replied slowly, "there is one other alternative you might try but it's not going to be easy."

"What is it, Doctor? We're willing to try anything."

"You must let the virus run its course and cease breeding for at least one year. Then, do a thorough antiviral cleaning of the facility and equipment. After all this is done, you can reintroduce breeding on a limited cycle."

The owners opted to try this method. Because they were most conscientious and followed the suggested procedures thoroughly, they were able to restart breeding with apparent control or possibly even the eradication of the disease. At the last report, several years later, all birds were healthy and breeding normally.

Will, the caller from Alaska, had one double yellow-headed Amazon parrot that was ill. He told me he had contacted nearby veterinarians but none of them had been able to help his parrot. After discussing the bird's symptoms with Will, I listed specific diagnostic tests that I needed performed by a local veterinarian and asked that, when they were completed, the veterinarian phone me with the results.

Two days later, I received the call. The bird had a minor bacterial infection and some nutritional deficiencies. I contacted the owner and discussed and outlined a treatment program. About three weeks later, I received a letter from Will, thanking me and saying the bird had responded and was now all right. As a way of expressing his gratitude, he enclosed a small statue of a typical Alaskan activity — a miner panning gold.

I first met Della when her attorney called me: He needed my help and could I please meet him at her house in an upper, middle class residential area in San Diego. He said that Animal Control had raided her home because neighbors had complained of the noise and the nuisance factor regarding the animals she had. No wonder the area residents had complained because Animal Control confiscated approximately one hundred dogs, mostly poodles, that she had living outside and inside the house.

It seems that Della was gone when Animal Control arrived with three vehicles and six to eight staff members. It took them several hours and several trips to load all the dogs into the trucks and deliver them to the main and outlying animal shelters.

When I arrived, Della and Tom, a friend of hers in his seventies and about ten years her senior, were cleaning up the yard and feeding approximately fifteen dogs, half of which were puppies. Apparently, these dogs were not taken during the raid because she had them with her in her motor home.

Della was furious and her attorney was trying to calm her but not succeeding. She felt her rights had been violated and what had happened was "unconstitutional" and were those of a "police state." She adamantly and repeatedly stated she had done nothing wrong, which un-doubtedly was why she was completely unprepared for the raid.

Her lawyer wanted my opinion regarding how competently she had cared for the confiscated animals in order to help him with her defense. With this in mind, I asked to see the house. Della took me on a tour, talking constantly about how she had done everything for her dogs, giving me detailed information on how she cared for them and assuring me that all were well fed. I know she truly felt she was doing her best. However, as we talked, I discov-ered she had neglected one very important item: vaccina-tions for each animal. This oversight would prove to be most disastrous for her pets during the next few days and months.

Because the dogs were placed in shelters with other animals, they were exposed to diseases and many of them died after a few days because they had not been immunized. As heartbreaking as this was, it helped the attorney establish a defense that the dogs must have been well-treated and were healthy because under her care, the death rate had been virtually nonexistent.

As I became more acquainted with Della and because of facts revealed in court and the newspapers, I learned about her background. She had been in a car accident many years ago that had damaged her physically and probably somewhat mentally. Because of this accident, she had received a large monetary settlement — enough to buy about twenty houses in various San Diego areas. It was fortunate that she had this real estate because as legal fees escalated, she was able to sell some of the houses to get money to continue to fight for the return of her animals.

Court procedures are notorious for dragging on and this one was no exception. Days turned into weeks, weeks into months and by the end of the case, about a year later, most of the dogs had either been euthanized or died. By the time the court ordered Animal Control to return the remaining animals, out of almost one hundred pets taken, only about thirty dogs were returned. If Della had won, it was a bittersweet victory.

Della owned a house on the outskirts of town that she decided to remodel just for her pets because she hoped animal control laws would be less stringent and there would be fewer neighbors to complain. She converted all the rooms into kennels and provided the animals with couches and chairs. She visited them daily and frequently spent the night with them.

Because she was a person who could not resist an animal, if she found a stray, she would take it home; if she passed a pet store and saw an appealing animal in the window, she would buy it and take it home. Soon, she had to keep her animals in two  houses because by now, the number of pets had doubled.

Just because she had moved to the suburbs and even though she had a minor win in court, it certainly did not mean her run-ins with officials were over. Animal Control, like the never-tiring IRS, continued to do inspections. Anytime she was inspected, the officer could easily find a discrepancy regarding sanitation because of the number of animals she kept. She would be cited and taken back to court. This continued for about six months until she bought a building, originally a pet hotel, near Mission Bay and close to my clinic. She was thrilled not only about her new place but now she could get a kennel license and keep all her pets legally. An exuberant Della called me to come over.

As I drove into the parking area, I could see that the exterior of the building was old and desperately in need of paint and repairs. Della greeted me at the door, smiling and so happy. She ushered me in and we toured the premises while she commented that the place needed some fixing up.

Indeed it did. The cement slab floors were cracked, the walls had holes in them, the linoleum on the floors was split and peeling and even the foundation had a hole in it where water could seep in. She was so ecstatic about her new place it was impossible for me to say what I really thought, "Burn it down and start all over. There's no way you can keep this place clean."

She must have used nearly all her remaining assets to buy this pet hotel so major improvements would be difficult if not impossible to accomplish. However, as the months went by, she was able to upgrade the building making it livable in a meager sense but, she was never able to convince Animal Control officers that she was keeping it in a suitable condition. Doubtlessly, part of this inability to satisfy the authorities stemmed from the animosity that existed between her and the officials that at this point was unsolvable.

She did a relatively good job of caring for the animals, now numbering somewhere between one hundred to one hundred and fifty. Most of the animals were hers but she also was boarding pets. Naturally, this led to other problems because the facility was disease ridden and impossible to sanitize. If a client brought her an animal to board and the animal had not been properly vaccinated, it could get viral diseases, parasites such as hook worms or anything else that the building harbored. The cats she boarded often fell ill to respiratory diseases.

She had a collection of birds that were maintained in good condition although the birds received less attention than the dogs and cats. There were a couple of scarlet macaws, a few Amazon parrots and a bunch of finches and canaries.

I treated her sick animals but relied on her to dispense any follow-up medication. Alas, she did not always follow my directions because she was one of those people who thought that if the required dosage was one pill, three or four would be better. I was called many times because of overdosing.

She set up a daily routine so that each animal would get special attention some time during the day. The kennel included spacious outdoor runs — although they were never too clean — where she would take them for a one-on-one encounter. This meant that with the number of animals she had, the routine required twenty-four hours a day, seven days a week. Fortunately, her friend Tom helped her. I suggested that she hire a full-time animal technologist to assist but she would not consider it. I also suggested she take her remaining money, leave and enjoy life a bit. "I'll never leave my animals," she replied.

Indeed, she loved her animals and the care she gave to this one animal proved it. She brought the black chow in to me because he was sick. I diagnosed the serious and usually fatal problem as distemper. For the sake of the  animal, I suggested it be euthanized because it would undoubtedly die. She absolutely refused and took it back to the kennel. An Animal Control officer on a routine inspection saw the dog, confiscated it and took it to a shelter. Della called me immediately, angry and upset. I quickly called the shelter. The veterinarian in charge felt about the animal as I did at first: It should be euthanized. I continued talking and finally convinced him that possibly the animal could survive but the only chance it had was under her care and she would give it the very best care.

Della got the animal back, continued caring for it diligently and eventually nursed it until it overcame most of the symptoms and its central nervous system problems caused by the disease. Although the dog was not one hundred percent cured — it had slight body tremors and a head tilt — it was able to function almost as well as a normal dog and, like most handicapped animals, was a loving pet.

This dog was one of the few animals I had ever seen that survived distemper and my only case where the owner was able to bring the dog through the disease. Just shows you what love, good care and perseverance can do.

Time went by and Della continued to have problems with Animal Control and, finally, her kennel license was revoked. After that, she was limited to the legal number of dogs she could have, six, but I am sure she never got down to that level. She closed her business and made plans to leave.

About a week before she left town, she came to the clinic and one of my staff took her into the examining room. When I walked in, I was surprised that she had no animal with her.

"What can I do for you?"

"I just want to give you something." She held out her hand, I extended mine and she put something in it. I looked down at a new one hundred dollar bill.

"What's this for?" I asked. "You don't owe me anything."

"You've been so good to me over the years, I wanted you to have it."

That was the last time I ever saw her. I have no idea where she went but I am sure that wherever she is, she is surrounded by animals.

8

The Unforgettable Vet

How long does an animal remember? Numerous of my cases show a pet remembers for years, for a lifetime.

An animal learns through its own trials and errors, its association with a person and how that individual treats or mistreats it and then remembers the occurrence. For example, if one uses a hand or foot to show disapproval, the animal will associate and remember that part of the body with a painful experience. This type of punishment is almost always counterproductive and does irreparable damage to the relationship between pet and owner.

Because most pets want to please their owners, a minimum of proper punishment usually produces a maximum of good behavior. Use a folded newspaper to reprimand a dog or cat because the animal then associates the paper, not a part of the body, with punishment. For a bird, a light spritzing of water from a spray bottle works well. Be sure the bottle is a different shape than the one used for bathing the bird because it will associate the container by its shape with a pleasant happening, bathing, for example, or an unpleasant one, punishment. When training his cockatoos, one bird owner client would throw a glassful of water at them when they were too noisy. Within a short time, the sight of the glass, even though it was empty, would bring immediate silence to the room.

Most animals learn throughout their lives and the adage, "You can't teach an old dog new tricks," is incorrect. Training, retraining and behavior modifications can be accomplished by interactive and remote punishment, aversion conditioning and, in extreme cases, psychoactive drugs, hormones and even surgery.

Unlike animal owners who can lavish great quantities of affection daily on a pet — a positive action — and administer punishment in small doses — a negative one — a veterinarian does what is necessary to keep or restore a pet's good health whether that animal views it as a plus or minus. Because of the lack of frequent contact and the ability to build up a long-term, trusting rapport, no matter how gently the necessary medication is administered or the treatment given, some animals tend to be extremely upset by the presence of a doctor. For this type of pet, a veterinarian is most unforgettable.

One bird who developed an outstanding memory for me was Pal, a double yellow-headed Amazon parrot, whose owners had lavished amenities on him. He had a private eight- by ten-foot carpeted room covered with a plastic drop cloth to protect it because he was never caged but always free to roam. The room had a window and planter box with expanded metal shelves, a television set and a four-foot high perch in the middle of the room. When he tired of looking out the window or watching TV, he had many toys to occupy his time and it was one of those toys that caused his surgery.

His bell was hanging by a chain that had links with an inside diameter as small as that of his toe instead of larger links where toes could enter and be withdrawn easily. Pal got one of his two front toes caught in a link, pulled and tugged until he got it out and while doing, stripped away all the gray, scaly skin and delicate flesh leaving only the bare bone exposed.

I knew as soon as I examined him what must be done. "I have to amputate that toe."

"Oh, dear," Mary lamented. "I'd hoped that perhaps the skin would grow back."

"I'm afraid not because this is more than just a scrape. All the tissue is gone."

"Will he be able to balance and stay on his perch all right with only one front toe?"

"Yes, he'll adapt in no time," I responded with reassurance.

I set up my operating area, grabbed him with a towel and my wife, who occasionally accompanied and helped me, held the bird while I administered a local anesthetic. As soon as the area was deadened, I removed the toe leaving enough skin to pull over the bone and to suture. In about ten minutes, he was back on his perch with a liquid bandage —

one a bird cannot pull off and that would last for several hours to a day — covering the area and he began to move about easily.

"Apply this topical medication as best you can several times a day," I said, "for as long as he'll let you."

With a puzzled look, Mary asked, "As long as he'll let me? What do you mean?"

"As Pal gets better, he'll start fighting you when you try to put on the medicine so, when it becomes impossible to treat him, discontinue using it. I think he'll be just fine but call me if you have any questions or problems."

I talked to Mary several times during the next few weeks getting positive progress reports but did not see Pal until about six months later when she called me out to check on her dog who had an ear infection. After treating Dusty, I asked, "Can I see Pal and how the surgery has healed?"

"Of course," she replied. "Come this way," she said as we walked the corridor. "You were right. The loss of that toe has not bothered him at all."

I stepped into Pal's room where he was on his t-bar perch, happily preening himself. He glanced up and when he saw me, started squawking and flew as quickly and as far away from me as he could, to the window and shelving. He grasped the underside of the shelf with his good foot and hung upside down, his back towards me. Immediately, he drew the foot with the missing toe close to his body and spread his wing over it to hide it and let loose a barrage of shrill screams and squawks that resounded throughout the room.

"Heavens," she exclaimed. "I've never heard him do that!"

"Well," I shouted over the ruckus, "obviously he remembers me and what I had to do."

Grandpa, an African gray parrot, had a serious defect called a scissors beak that occurs when the upper part of the beak does not meet the lower one but slices over it, like a pair of scissors. This condition is often caused by a nutritional deficiency, especially an inadequate level of calcium that sometimes is found in birds who eat only seeds.

I explained the possible causes of his scissors beak, the time and fees involved to attempt to fix it and that even with treatment, I might not be able to correct his bite. However, without attempting to repair it, this condition could shorten his expected life span.

"Please, Doctor Ewing," Ann said, her forehead wrinkled with concern, "try to help him. We love him so much and want to give him the best chance possible to be our companion for many years to come."

I laid out my instruments on the table, captured him and took a blood sample. I suspected, judging by his mis-shapen beak, that he was in poor health.

"Gradually, I can reshape his beak — the result of the problem — but we need to deal with what has caused the scissors beak in the first place. You must change his seed diet to a nutritionally balanced pelleted food to improve his overall condition and strengthen his beak. Several such products are on the market, however, I developed one, Bird Life, that I feel is exceptionally well-balanced and nutritional. Slowly introduce him to his new food but switch him over as soon as you can."

"Of course, Doctor. I never realized a seed diet could be harmful to a bird. I thought that's what all birds were supposed to eat."

Ann left the room, still mumbling about diets as I caught the bird in a towel and placed him on his side on the table. My wife, again acting as an assistant, held the bird in the towel while I began working on his beak. With a Dremel tool, I cautiously sculptured the upper and lower beak in the direction which they should go then smoothed them with emery boards. In about thirty minutes, I had shaped his beak as much as I could during this first session.

When the laboratory diagnosis of the blood sample arrived two days later, it confirmed what I had thought about Grandpa's condition. I called Ann with these results and again stressed the importance of changing his diet.

"I've already begun adding some of the new food and he's eating it. Another few days and I think he'll be entirely off of seeds and on the pelleted food."

"That's good," I replied, pleased that she had begun the changeover so quickly. "The sooner you can switch him completely, the better for him."

Two months later, I visited Grandpa to sculpture the beak again. I entered the room and when he saw me, he started making growling and clucking noises. Disregarding his unfriendly welcome, I captured him and did another blood test. By simply looking at him, he appeared to be responding to his new diet because his overall physical condition had improved. As I ground and filed the area, I thought about his improvement and the pleasant idea that maybe I just might be able to correct the scissors beak after all.

Three more months passed and it was time for another beak shaping. Again, as I entered the room, Grandpa made growling and clucking sounds only this time, more loudly and often than the last.

Ann, amazed by his noises, commented, "He never makes those sounds except when you are near. You certainly have made a lasting impression on him!"

Visits became farther apart during the next months but always Grandpa displayed the same threatening, greeting procedure. By the end of the seventh year, testing showed that with the pelleted diet he was healthy and, along with my numerous sculpting jobs, he no longer had a scissors beak. The last time I saw Grandpa, about eight years after that first visit, he still remembered me. As I approached him, he continuously squawked a loud clucking, guttural unfriendly welcome that he used only with me.

Does a change of environment effect an animal's ability to remember a person? Joey was an eighteen-inch long, two-toned green military macaw that showed me the answer.

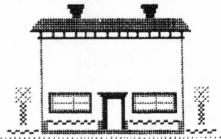

I had been to Sharon Tanner's apartment three or more times to check Joey and trim his wings and nails. When capturing any bird needing medical treatment or a beak and toenail trim, I wrap the bird quickly in a towel because, although beaks give painful pinches, I get more cuts from razor-sharp nails than beaks. And, unless the bird gets sick, I usually only see it when the nails have grown out to a skin-slicing length again.

In Joey's case, I needed to be exceptionally swift because with each visit, Joey became more and more aggressive. As soon as he saw me, he rapidly headed to the open cage door and lunged with beak open and cutting nails ready to claw. However, I had an edge over these speedy attacks because, although some birds may take a zigzag course towards me, without exception, he attacked only in a "zig" pattern.

Sharon had called and set up an appointment for trimming Joey's beak and nails. I arrived at the scheduled time and knocked on the door with my medical case in hand.

"Hello, Doctor Ewing," she said, welcoming me. "Please come in."

"Hi. How's Joey doing?" I inquired as I walked into the living room, set the case down and opened it to get the necessary clippers and towel. I knew that when dealing with Joey, I had to be ready for his attack before I entered the family room where he was.

"He's fine but something puzzles me," she said. "Joey is such a sweet, loving bird with me and all my friends. I don't understand why he acts so nasty towards you."

"Well," I smiled, "I guess he doesn't like what I do to him."

"It's quite clear, he certainly remembers you. You don't hurt him, do you? I mean grabbing him in that towel, he looks like he's suffocating all wrapped up in it. He can breathe, can't he?"

Joey may have been predictable when it came to his attacks but so was Sharon when it came to conversation. Each time I treated Joey, she asked the same questions and always was overly concerned that I would hurt her beloved pet. Sharon, however, was not unique in her apprehensive attitude because many animal owners become distraught when their pet shows displeasure and fearful that the racket it makes indicates unnecessary pain or that the pet is "surely going to die."

Another upset owner who I also had to reassure constantly while working on her bird was positive it would hate her after its clipping. Instead, each time I finished, it went directly to her, wanting to be caressed and was outwardly affectionate to her. When dealing with such pet owners, I sometimes spend more time talking to and massaging the nerves of the owners than it takes to treat the animal.

"Of course," I continued patiently, as if I had never been asked these questions before, "he can breathe and actually, the towel seems to have a calming effect that a bird is willing to accept when wrapped in it. Plus, it's the safest way for the bird — and the vet."

"Wouldn't it be better if you wore gloves?" she asked, still unconvinced that I was not going to hurt her bird.

"No," I explained one more time. "If I wore gloves, I would lose the sense of feeling and could not tell how firmly I was holding him. Birds do not have a diaphragm so they breathe with their rib cage. If I wore gloves and accidentally squeezed him too hard, he could suffocate quickly and I wouldn't know it. By wrapping a towel loosely around his body, I can feel him breathing and check if his heart beat is good and his respiration solid. I often place a glove or any other similarly heavy material between his head and my hand or arm because he can't bite through it like he can a towel."

I could tell by the look on her face, she still had doubts. "Let's give Joey his much needed trim," I said, beaming a bolstering smile.

Like a matador with cape in hand, I with my towel, strode confidently in to meet my adversary. Once the cage door was opened, Joey made his predictable assault as swiftly as any charging bull. I held the towel exactly where I knew he would head and, as in the past, he shot

into it. I had him securely wrapped before he had the chance to bite or claw me.

"Did you hurt him? It looked like you grabbed him too hard. Is he in pain? It sounds like you hurt him." She twisted the ring on her finger back and forth anxiously. "Oh, dear, I'm so upset!"

"No, he's just fine, aren't you, Joey?" Joey squawked with displeasure. With each clip or trim, Sharon bombarded me with cautioning comments or leery questions and Joey with baby-talking soothing statements. The noisier the bird was, the more panicky she became.

With all the bird sounds and the running, reassuring commentary for Sharon's benefit, the routine trimming seemed to take an hour when actually Joey was back in his cage in about twenty minutes. Now that she could see her pet was alive and all right, she sighed with relief and smiled for the first time since I arrived.

"Thank you so much, Doctor," she said while walking me to the door. "I'm so glad that's over for another few months."

"You're welcome." I waved and headed towards the motor home. Although she may have been glad that it was over, I was exuberant.

Several months passed before I heard from Sharon. She called to make an appointment for Joey's routine trimming, informed me she had moved and gave me directions to her new apartment. I wondered as I drove there if Joey would be as belligerent in new surroundings as he was in his old home. Would a change of location bring a change of attitude?

I entered and, uncertain as to whether his attitude may or may not have changed, prepared as I had done in the past. Good thinking on my part! The second Joey saw me, he squawked loudly and savagely lunged in the same, unfriendly manner he used only with me.

Sharon moved two more times and no matter where she lived, Joey always behaved the same towards me. My conclusion from Joey's behavior is that, yes, a bird remembers a person and this recognition has nothing to do with the bird's surroundings.

Samantha and Tabitha were declawed seal point Siamese house cats that remembered not a particular veterinarian but who had a hatred for all veterinarians in general. The first time Carol McCall phoned me, she was quite honest when explaining her feline companions ugly attitude towards doctors.

"Doctor Ewing, I must tell you before you come out, no vet has been able to handle them without getting bitten severely. They are wonderful pets except when it comes to a doctor. I must warn you, they can be most vicious and you may not want to treat them, you may not want to come out. But — I hope you will because," she said with despair tingeing each word, "you are about my last hope."

"Wouldn't it be easier if you took them to a clinic, rather than having me come to your house?" I inquired.

"I wish it were that simple but they absolutely refuse to travel. I can't even get them into a carrying cage."

"Certainly I'll come. I think I can handle them. I've treated numerous hard to deal with cases before," I replied with confidence.

As I drove to her Escondido home, I thought of other owners who had mentioned that their pet or pets were almost impossible for a veterinarian to cope with. After I had successfully treated the pet, they were amazed that I had been able to do it. I have never known why — could it be luck or were my hands big enough to grasp them firmly yet caringly or was it the comforting way in which I spoke or did I have some kind of mysterious soothing affect on otherwise unruly animals? I have never been certain why I seem to succeed where others had failed but whatever the reason, I hoped that special quality was with me this day: A cat bites very deeply, very quickly and the wound is very painful.

As soon as the front door was opened, I saw the cats in the living room, contentedly lounging while licking to clean themselves. Each looked up, saw me and my medical kit and, as fast as jet-propelled missiles, streaked from the room.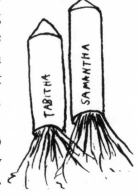

Had I forgotten to mention to Carol that to expedite the necessary treatment, she should have them contained in a small room, preferably the bathroom, or was I early and she had not had a chance to do it? No matter; now we would have to locate and corner them some way.

Carol ushered me in, saying, "I'm so glad you understand their temperaments and still would come out. They both need a checkup and vaccinations. I hope you're able to do it." Ralph, her husband, nodded his head in agreement.

"Well, I'm certainly going to try," I grinned as I replied. "First, though, we're going to have to find them. I saw them running down the corridor. Do they have favorite hiding places?"

"None in particular." We headed down the hall, Carol and Ralph calling out their names, as we began a room-to-room search, lifting bedspread edges, looking under beds, inside open clothes closets, behind bookcases and pulling floor length draperies aside.

In the last room, under the queen-sized bed and as close to the unreachable center of the mattress as possible were the cowering medical candidates. They immediately hissed threatening warnings with teeth bared, ears laid back and eyes half-closed forming unfriendly slits. I chuckled as I flashed on the title of a book I had read written by a house call veterinarian specializing in cats — *All My Patients Are Under the Bed*. How appropriate!

Now to herd them into an area where I could catch them. The three of us, arms spread and flailing, maneuvered them toward the bathroom. I softly called out each ones name and before we had reached the bathroom, Tabitha had come to me.

"That's wonderful!" Carol exclaimed. "I've never seen her go willingly to a vet."

I picked up the soft and trembling cat. "Nice kitty. Nice Tabitha," I said to her as I ran my hands over her body, feeling for anything unusual.

"I'll go ahead with Tabitha's exam and vaccinations and you get Samantha into the bathroom."

By the time I had finished with Tabitha, the owners had Samantha confined. I opened the door slowly and saw the cat, crouching in the corner. She hissed, spit and drew back her lips exposing her knife-sharp teeth. She looked most fearsome but I knew that she was merely frightened and using the only defensive tactics she knew.

"Pretty Samantha. Come here girl. Nice Sam." I did not think she would come to me but, I hoped the cooing pleasantries might soothe her as with Tabitha. No such luck. She darted to the most inaccessible area in the bathroom — behind the toilet.

Although confining an animal in a small area like this four- by six-foot bathroom puts it within close reach and gives it fewer hiding places, for a person of my build — six-foot-two and about 200 pounds with a size eleven five E shoe — the room gave little space for me to stand in comfortably let alone maneuver easily. Because, allowing for the built-ins and permanent facilities, the actual remaining floor dimensions were about two- by four-feet. The challenge of catching the cat might be surpassed by the difficulty of trying not to trip over my own feet.

I placed a towel over my left hand, held the syringe in the other and stepped forward. I bent over extending the toweled hand around the toilet bowl trying to grab her long enough to administer the injection and, like many cornered, frightened animals, she urinated and defecated as she slipped away. Now I had to not only capture her but try to keep her from getting dirty in the mess she had created.

During the following fifteen minutes, we danced around the room making thumps and bangs accentuated by throaty hisses and my pacifying comments. By the commotion we were making, the owners standing on the other side of the door must have wondered who was winning and if they were  going to have to call in a repairman to fix any damages or get out a medical kit to repair my wounds.

Again, she squeezed in between the toilet and wall. I quickly bent over and grasped her head with the toweled hand on one side of the bowl, reached around the other side of it and plunged the syringe into her hind quarter, just under the skin. Done! I stood, breathed a sigh of success, cautiously opened the door so she would not get out and left.

"Could you catch her?" Ralph asked.

"Yes," I smiled and wiped the perspiration from my forehead. "As you probably noted, it wasn't easy and you do have a mess in the bathroom and a cat that needs washing before letting her out. I tried the best I could to keep her away from the soiled area but — "

"That's all right," Carol interrupted. "Don't worry. We're just pleased that she got her shot. Thanks so much for everything. And, you're the first vet that has ever been able to touch Tabitha without her putting up a fight and you actually managed to get Samantha, too. You definitely are good with cats."

I smiled, flattered by her comment, closed my medical bag and prepared to leave. "Thanks. My staff frequently has mentioned that I do have a way with cats." As I walked out the door I said, "Give me a call if I can help you again."

Several months passed before I had a request from Carol. This time, however, it was not for a routine checkup: Samantha was sick and would I please come out.

"Of course, and," recalling my last encounter with Samantha, "please have her in the bathroom when I get there."

"Certainly. We'll see you tomorrow."

It really did not matter if she was in confined quarters this time because she was so ill that she laid listlessly on the bathroom floor, unable to muster more than a halfhearted hiss when I entered. She let me pick her up without a fight and her limp body only quivered slightly with fear.

"Poor, Samantha," I murmured softly to her as I caringly ran my hands over her.

"I'm afraid I'm going to have to take her with me," I said to Carol, "and run some tests to find out exactly what is wrong." I put her in the carrying cage and headed to the front door. "I'll call you when I get the results. Don't worry. I'm sure she'll be fit in no time."

I carried her into the clinic, removed her from the portable cage and placed her in our small animal cage. Although she was in a debilitated state, she still was spunky enough to require a tranquilizing shot in order to get the necessary blood samples.

During the hospital stay and treatment for a bacterial infection, she was not exactly the perfect patient but, considering her actions when she was at home, she was fairly easy to handle. Perhaps she behaved better here during her two day stay because she was not strong enough to fight or because she felt insecure in unfamiliar surroundings or, I hoped, maybe she had changed her feelings towards veterinarians.

Carol called about six months later requesting that I come out because it was time for vaccinations and checkups for the two cats again. I wondered as I drove to their house how Samantha would act. Would she remember me as someone who made her feel better — or had her previous hatred of veterinarians returned?

The answer was obvious the moment I stepped into the bathroom. She snarled, hissed, flattened her ears and bared her teeth. Samantha was definitely her old self! With the towel in my left hand and syringe in the right, we began again our rowdy, clamorous chase-and-catch routine.

Extremely Exotic

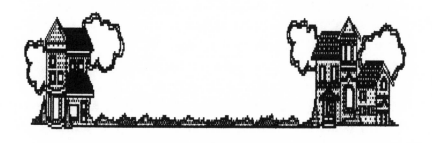

It had been a routine house call day. I had trimmed birds' nails and beaks, discussed skin conditions and flea problems with dog and cat owners and now, at my last stop, called my answering machine. No messages so I could leave from here and go home to dinner. Hmm. Dinner. I was starving and could almost smell the aroma of baked chicken that I had been promised for supper.

I walked into my house and deeply inhaled the delicious odor wafting from the kitchen. "Hi, I'm home. Smells wonderful and I'm famished. I'll be there as soon as I check the answering machine." What a mistake that was. I should have eaten first.

The light on the machine was blinking. I pushed the playback message button and — "Doctor Ewing, you don't know me but I got your name from a neighbor of mine, Pete Fletcher, the one whose cockatiels you took care of. He said you did unusual cases — er, animals, that is. I have a twelve-year-old pet boa constrictor that I've raised since he was a baby and something is wrong, terribly wrong. I'm worried sick." The concern in the man's voice was obvious. "Would you please call me immediately. My name is Jay Beltcher and my number is 555-6123. Please — call immediately."

I picked up the phone and dialed. Jay filled me in on the symptoms and I felt I had to see the snake as soon as possible. "I'll be there in thirty minutes."

I walked towards the front door, yelling over my shoulder, "Got an emergency, have to leave. Go ahead and eat but save something for me. I'll eat when I get back."

My, my another meal missed. I got into the car and reached immediately for my cache of candy bars in the glove box, kept there for evenings like this. Not exactly a health food but at least it would keep my stomach from growling. "I should have bought stock in Snickers," I said aloud while mentally counting the number of candy bars I had eaten instead of meals during the last few months.

As I approached the end of the cul-de-sac where Jay lived, I could see a man who had to be Jay, pacing back and forth in front of the garage. I pulled into the driveway and he rushed to open the car door for me.

"This way, Doctor." He ushered me promptly into the garage where a wire mesh cage on a platform about two feet off the cement floor stretched along one side of the garage. It was about fifteen-feet long by five-feet high by five-feet wide with an entry at one end. What a great setup for a snake!

There, inside the cage, lethargically lay Oscar the boa. I walked along the outside of the cage looking in at him. I guessed he was more than ten-feet long, weighed about eighty pounds and had a girth of about twelve to fourteen inches at his widest area. Hardly a wimpy garter snake. His sleek, smooth pale brown skin with dark crosswise bars appeared in good condition.

"As I mentioned on the phone," Jay said, "Oscar has been listless for two or three days. Usually, he comes to me when I call him and he loves being handled. When I'm out here, he watches my every move and everything that is going on. But, now he is totally unresponsive. This is definitely not his normal behavior."

"Have there been any changes in his diet or feeding routine?"

"No," Jay answered, shaking his head.

"Would Oscar let me handle him?" I asked.

"I'm sure he wouldn't mind. Especially since he's not feeling good."

I put the stethoscope around my neck, picked up the speculum in case I needed to pry open Oscar's mouth and placed my magnifying visor on my head. I stooped over, climbed into the cage and began to slowly crawl alongside his partially stretched out body. And, I do mean slowly because to crawl on knees surgically mended to help correct problems created by playing basketball for too many years was not an easy task.

Once I reached his head, I was able to sit up which relieved some of the knee discomfort but I certainly do not recommend this pseudo-Lotus position I was forced to assume to anyone with debilitated joints. I reached over and gently touched his head to see if he would respond. He moved slightly. I lifted his head and, without the help of the speculum, opened his mouth expecting to see some condition indicating a sick snake. I was surprised when his mouth and throat looked normal. I checked his eyes, the condition of the scales, his ears and nose and his over all muscle tone. All seemed fine.

Oscar began to stir a bit and it was obvious he was having difficulty moving. I continued his examination by running my hands down his body. Everything seemed okay except for what might be a mild swelling in the area of his respiratory system. I held my stethoscope over this area and thought I detected a rale, a gurgling sound that is an audible symptom of an infection. I sat next to Oscar, held his head and watched him breathe for about five minutes.

In order to find out exactly what Oscar's problem was, I needed a specimen to culture and I felt taking it from the oral cavity would not give me the necessary material to examine because the enlargement and lung area were too far from the throat. I asked Jay to give me the syringe and needle I had placed on top of the medical kit, just in case I needed it. He handed it to me through a wire mesh opening and I did a needle puncture into the swelling. I backed out of the cage, with only a few groans, gratefully stood up and gently shook each leg to get the circulation going again.

I knew, unfortunately, that the lab generally takes two or three days to get the results from the tests and I felt the boa's condition needed immediate medication. For most animals, antibiotics are usually not hazardous but for a snake, they can be a risky undertaking because of the side effects that include kidney toxicity — a killer for reptiles and birds. In addition, most research and development of medications are based on mammals and to convert dosages to reptiles, birds or any exotic animal can be difficult and dangerous. However, I felt that if I did not prescribe something now, the snake might die before I had the results: I thought I might be dealing with an organism that would kill Oscar if left unchecked.

I discussed Oscar's condition and the pros and cons of antibiotics for reptiles with the anxious owner and concluded, "I think that we should give Oscar an injection of a suitable broad spectrum antibiotic now, before the culture results come back."

Jay hesitated only a moment before agreeing with me. He, too, felt that the possible benefits of the medication outweighed the risks involved.

"Oscar will need two injections a day. Can you give them?" I asked.

"Sure," Jay replied. "I belong to the local reptile association and I've helped members give injections to their pets. I know I can give Oscar his."

Through past experiences and results with birds, reptiles and mammals, I estimated the proper dosage for a reptile of his size. I used an antibiotic with the highest probability of success against the organism I suspected was causing Oscar's illness. I gave Oscar his first injection through the wire cage and left Jay with enough antibiotic and syringes to last for the next three days.

"I'm anxious to get this specimen to the lab. I'll call you tomorrow to see how Oscar's doing." I drove immediately to the County Veterinary Laboratory, deposited the specimen in the refrigerated, exterior drop box and headed home, hoping that I had calculated right on the medication and the amount to be given.

I called Jay early the next day. "How's Oscar?"

"Well, I don't really see any change."

I breathed a quiet sigh of relief. At least the boa was not dead. "It's a little soon for the antibiotic to take effect. I'll call you tomorrow to see if there's any change."

During my lunch break, I went to the lab and talked to the microbiologist, explaining the importance of the results of the culture. I told her what I thought might be there and to culture for these things. She thought she could expedite the results, in fact, maybe even have them by the next morning.

My first phone call of that day was the lab and my original suspicions were correct. Oscar had a deadly bacteria called *pseudomonas aeruginosa* that is generally resistant to antibiotics. The culture and sensitivity plate showed which antibiotics the organism was sensitive to and that I had administered the proper one. I was greatly relieved.

I called Jay. "We've got the results back and we're giving the right antibiotic." I explained what Oscar had. "I'd like to come out this afternoon, take another look at Oscar and alter the dosages slightly."

When I arrived at Jay's, he was waiting for me, smiling happily. "Good news," he beamed. "Oscar seems better this afternoon."

"That's wonderful." I grinned, also pleased with this progress report.

We walked into the garage and I could see that the boa was moving around some and was definitely more interested in what was happening outside his cage. He was beginning to show signs of recovery.

I increased the dosage due to the findings. "Continue the inoculations twice a day for the next three days. It will be normal for Oscar to drink more water and to excrete more urine due to the antibiotics. Call me if there are any problems. If I don't hear from you, I'll be out at the end of the three days to check him over."

Oscar had no further problems within those days and he seemed to be progressing well when I examined him. I told Jay to stop giving the medication for two weeks and then continue with another five-day session and be sure to call if there was anything suspicious.

A month later, Oscar was doing fine. About three months later, simply because I was curious to see how he was doing, I stopped by Jay's on my way home. When Oscar saw me, he crawled over towards the edge of the cage. I reached a finger through the cage and patted him on the top of the head.

Was he just being his usual inquisitive self, I wondered, or did he remember me as someone who had done something to make him feel better? How often I had thought, if only my patients could speak.

I had already been on a house call to see her military macaws but this time Michelle wanted me to examine her two green iguanas and probably give them a nail trim. As soon as I arrived, she ushered me to a second floor bedroom outfitted to please even the most discriminating iguana. The synthetic tree branches stretched from the linoleum-covered floor to the ceiling and climbing poles made especially for them wound their way upward. On the floor was a plastic bin filled with water for drinking or an occasional wallow. The spacious walk-in closet was their den where they had a box big enough to crawl and hide in without being cramped and a wire cage large enough to be comfortable in if it was necessary to contain them. Two "hot rocks" used for keeping reptiles warm on chilly days sat on the floor.

I got a quick glimpse of the iguanas before they retreated to the closet, trying to hide from me, a stranger. Each was about three feet long with two-thirds of the body being tail. Mature iguanas of this species are brown in color but they were still green indicating they were youngsters.

I talked to the owner for a while, inquiring about the iguanas' general health. Michelle said that they seemed fine but she would just like me to check them over to make sure.

"What are you feeding them?"

"They like many things so I vary their diet. They get a combination of dandelion flowers and leaves, thawed frozen vegetables, fresh fruit, crickets, an occasional baby mouse, cooked eggs, meal worms and small amounts of dog food."

Not only did they have palatial accommodations, they ate like kings, too. "No wonder they look so healthy," I said.

By now, curiosity had the better of one of the iguanas. He or she — at this age, there is little difference between the appearance of a male or female — had crept out on a branch where I could get close enough to pick it up. I ran my hands over its scaly body, down the crest running the length of the back, examined the dewlap under the chin and looked into its bright bead-like eyes. It appeared quite fit but definitely needed its nails trimmed.

I removed the clippers from my pocket and started cutting the nails on each of its long, thin toes. Other than whipping its tail a bit, it did not seem to mind the pedicure, in fact, it looked like it enjoyed the attention. By the time I had finished with this one and placed it back on the branch, the other one, creeping slowly and inquisitively, was close enough to pick up and inspect. I placed it on my lap and gave it a similar examination and nail trim.

"There you are," I smiled at Michelle. "They seem to be in good condition. Keep up your excellent care and they should be around for a long time. Iguanas in captivity have been known to live fifteen or more years."

Some reptilian pets are so unique, such as this Australian skink that Madeline was bringing in to me, that I had to rush to my reference books before she arrived. Although I had handled skinks in the past, I had not had an occasion to treat one and, as you might guess, none of my books had any information on those that come from Down Under.

Madeline placed the animal in its cage on the examining table. One quick glance was all I needed to know that it did not look healthy because its skin, instead of being somewhat moist, was extremely dry.

Elmer, the skink, definitely needed attention.

As I looked at him, I was reminded of one of our southwestern desert dwellers, the Gila monster. This Australian cousin had a similar beaded pattern but with an overall blackish appearance, speckled with brown and beige. He was about fifteen-inches long with a fat three- to four-inch midsection and a short tail, hardly a tail at all when compared to that of an iguana.

I lifted Elmer out of the cage, inspecting him while I ran my fingers over his body. His skin felt bumpy, similar to the texture of a woman's beaded purse. He obviously was not feeling good because every time I poked him even a little, he winced. A healthy reptile in captivity is used to being touched and usually ignores minor prodding. Externally, I did not see anything out of the ordinary except for the poor condition of his skin. I took a stool sample and a throat swab to check for organisms.

"I need to do some further research on a proper nutritional program for Elmer because I think that may be one reason for his dry skin condition. I'll call you later today and let you know what I've found." As I spoke, I was covering Elmer's body with a moisturizing, medicated lotion. "I know we can help him immediately by using this lotion." I handed her the tube. "Put it on him two to three times a day."

Madeline and Elmer left for her car and I headed for the telephone and more research. I called several colleagues who had good ideas and then Doctor Phil Ensley at the San Diego Zoo who gave me a great deal of pertinent information regarding the general care of skinks.

I compiled all my findings, called Madeline and discussed the procedures I thought would benefit Elmer. I recommended cleaning the animal often with warm water in order to add more moisture, using the moisturizing lotion and attempting to balance his food intake. He could have fruit flies, crickets, eggs, a small amount of dog food and pieces of fruits and vegetables.

In two weeks, Madeline returned with Elmer who was beginning to look quite handsome — for a skink, that is. His skin was almost back to a normal condition and he was more inquisitive.

"Elmer is definitely responding to his moisturizing program and new diet. Unless something unusual occurs, I don't think I need to see him again."

Three months later, Madeline was in to see me with her dog who had a skin problem. "How's Elmer doing?" I inquired while checking the dog.

Madeline burst into tears. Between sobs and blowing her nose she managed to tell me the sad finale of Elmer. She had to go out of town so left him with a friend. Somehow or another Elmer's heat rock malfunctioned and probably he was electrocuted, the friend did not know for sure.

I was sad for both Elmer and Madeline, particularly because of the way the animal died. Unfortunately, this tragic ending is not uncommon because cold-blooded animals such as lizards, snakes, skinks, turtles and iguanas generally require a source of heat. Indoors, this usually means some type of an electrically controlled heating device. Owners need to be as careful with these objects around pets as they are with electrical appliances around toddlers because animals can be just as curious.

Make sure the animal cannot get caught inside the appliance and become trapped. Be sure there are no loose electrical wires or connections that the animal can get tangled in. Actually, in most cases, it is best to have a heating system, preferably thermostatically controlled, that uses light bulbs and is placed a safe distance from the animal.

One of the meanings of the word exotic is "strange or different in a way that is striking or fascinating." Without a doubt, these two varieties of birds are exotic: emus and rheas. Emus and rheas are some of the members of a group called ratites that are large, flightless birds with a flat breastbone instead of the keel-like ridge that flying birds have. Both have small wings, useless except for steering sharp corners while eluding predators. Both have three toes with sharp nails on each foot.

Emus stand six-feet tall and are the world's second largest bird with only the eight-foot ostrich being bigger. They are native to Australia's grassy plains and open forests and their long frond-like plumage is gray to brown and more closely resembles coarse hair than feathers. They are good swimmers and excellent runners, able to go thirty miles an hour. And, they have an unquenchable curiosity that can get themselves — or others — into trouble.

Rheas, who are native to the grasslands of South America, look like ostriches that have shrunk in the wash and then been fluffed in a dryer. The common rhea can grow to five-feet tall and is the biggest bird in the New World. Their brownish, fluffy feathers are used commercially for dusters. Like the emu, the rhea is a good swimmer and a fast runner, able to outrun a horse.

When I first decided to specialize in avian medicine, I had no idea that sometime in the future, I would have an opportunity to treat such large and interesting patients. But as I became more well-known in the avian field, I guess it was only natural for clients to call me to care for a bird whether it weighed a few ounces or hundreds of pounds.

A client from a San Diego beach area phoned me to come out to do a routine check of his pet emu. The owner

kept Big Bird in the back yard that was enclosed by a
six-foot high, vine-covered fence and bordered an alley on
one side. The owner and I chatted for a while, discussing
the emu's diet, bedding, housing, exercise program — in
general, all about Big Bird's care. As we talked, the emu's
shyness with a stranger was overcome by his curiosity and
he strolled over, stopping next to me.

I reached my hand out and patted him. He did not
seem to mind being touched in the least. With such a
cooperative patient, the exam would not be as difficult as I
had imagined it might be. I examined his beak which felt
hard and somewhat like an animal's horn, I looked in the
ear holes on each side of his head for any abnormalities and
then I opened his mouth and looked at his large fleshy
tongue. All appeared normal.

His feathers were easily compressed so I could feel
any lumps that might be on his body underneath the
feathers. I parted a feathered area and looked at his skin
which resembled that of a chicken. He did not seem to mind
when I ran my hands down his scaly legs and, as I stooped
to examine his toes and nails, he arched his neck, cocking
his head to one side and watched closely as if he was truly
fascinated by my every movement.

I had just finished, when we heard a noisy motorcycle coming down the alley. In three giant steps, Big Bird
was at the fence, looking over it to see what was happening.
From the alley side, only his head peered out from above
the fence and, like a turning periscope, he followed the roar
of the cycle.

Wham! Crash! Smashing noises were followed by loud expletives.

I dashed to the wall and looked over. The black tire skid marks led to the motorcycle that was on its side amidst garbage cans and trash. The swearing biker, stood and brushed the dirt off his leather jacket and pants.

"Are you all right?" I yelled.

"Yeah. But what the *!* was that?"

"It's an emu, a big, harmless bird."

Big Bird blinked his brown eyes as he inquisitively watched the man struggle to right his bike.

"A bird! Thank God. I thought I was being attacked by a cobra!"

I was called to an emu ranch located outside of San Diego and maintained by the Scripps Foundation because one of the flock was injured. Apparently, something had spooked an emu, it had tried to go through a fence and fractured its eight-inch long wing-like limb. The big question was, how do you splint such a small appendage on such a big bird?

After much thought, observing the bird from every direction and a lengthy discussion about the situation with the manager, Bob, we decided the only practical way for the wing to properly heal was to totally immobilize it by securing it to the body of the bird. And, unlike Big Bird who was used to being touched and pampered, this emu was wild. Bob managed to shoo the bird into a corner of the enclosure while I went to my medical case to get a special self-adhering elastic bandage, ideal for such purposes.

These bandages are purchased in large batches and are quite patriotic in color: red, white or blue. Unfortunately for the emu, the only color I had with me was red. Bob held the bird as best he could while I began winding the vibrantly colored material around the bird's body with the injured wing flattened to its side and then around the front legs . . . and then around and around and around again. I stepped back to admire my handiwork and, goodness, what a sight. The emu, outfitted in this fancy crimson coat, looked as if it were ready for a formal New Year's Eve party. All that was missing was a top hat and bow tie!

I was concerned that the bird would try to peck or pick the bandage off during the time necessary for healing but according to the manager, it did not pay any attention to it. At the end of ten days when the emu's wing had healed, I returned to the ranch and removed the bandage. The tiny appendage seemed as mobile and in as good a condition as the uninjured one and just as useless, exactly like it was supposed to be.

About a month later, I was called out because another emu had done the same thing. Now that I was an "expert" in emu wing immobilization, I knew exactly what to do. I dug into my medical case, pulled out the roll of red bandage and started to work.

Marilyn phoned me to come to her rhea ranch near Ramona because two of her twelve birds were sick. She told me the birds seemed listless and although there was no feather loss, they fluffed their feathers like sick birds do.

As we walked the short distance from the main house to the building where the birds were kept, she told me she had been raising rheas for two years. This was the first time she had had any problems with them and she was not sure exactly what was wrong.

The two ill birds were in a separate holding pen away from the healthy birds and I could see by the way they stood, something was not right. In addition, they did not put up much of a struggle when I tried to examine them as untamed ones should have done. A close look at the feathers showed lice but I did not think this finding was sufficient for the symptoms they had. Something more had to be wrong.

I collected fecal droppings and did swabs of the upper throat for diagnoses while Marilyn answered my questions about their nutrition and general husbandry as well as sanitation procedures used at the ranch. Because it was early enough for me to get the samples to the laboratory, I decided not to start them on any medication until I knew exactly what I was dealing with.

I left the ranch and went directly to the lab, asked the microbiologist to examine for internal parasites and do a routine culture and sensitivity plate for infectious organisms. She told me she could do the parasite exam immediately so I decided to wait for the results.

The diagnosis was coccidiosis and round worms, two conditions that could cause the symptoms I had seen. Coccidiosis, a parasitic intestinal disease of protozoan origin found frequently in zoos, is transmitted in the feces. It causes diarrhea sometimes with blood, dehydration, depression, weakness and often can be difficult to clear up. Round worms are a common parasitic disease that are easier to control than coccidiosis.

I called Marilyn with the findings and she came down that afternoon to pick up the medicine for the rheas. The lab called the next day and said the culture was negative for pathogenic organisms which meant we were dealing only with the lice and the intestinal parasites. The previously prescribed medications should be all that were needed.

Within a few days, the rheas were showing marked signs of improvement. But, to make sure the diseases were under control, I tested them again in one month and the results showed they were parasite free. I suggested she have the rheas tested annually and that any new birds be examined and tested before introducing them into the flock. I told her about better ways to handle the flock's sanitation conditions because improper cleaning and disinfecting probably was the main cause of spreading the parasites.

The elderly white-haired woman in Poway escorted me into her double-wide mobile home. "I'm worried about Bootsie. She looks like she's losing weight. Am I feeding her the right things?"

I could see Bootsie, a Taiwanese pheasant, strutting around the other half of the mobile home through a gated doorway. She looked very much like the female ring-necked pheasant introduced here in the States from Asia. She was buff colored and about twenty inches in length from her head to her long tail.

What a lucky bird! The half of the house she was in was her domain; Maude lived in the other half. Maude, who spent a lot of time in the kitchen, had even fixed a ledge for Bootsie above the sink and on the bird's side of the wall so that the bird could sit there and Maude could talk to her while she worked.

I opened the gate and Maude and I entered. Under Bootsie's shelf was a large container cage, just in case the bird needed to be kept from mischief while Maude was gone. In one corner were her food and water bowl and the floor was covered with newspapers to make cleanup easy.

Maude called the pheasant's name and Bootsie came running right to us. I reached down and picked her up, running my hands over her feathers, feeling for any bumps or abnormalities. She seemed fine. I sat her down and she sped to Maude who picked her up, snuggling the bird in her arms.

"How old is Bootsie?" I asked.

"About fourteen," she said as she stroked Bootsie. "I've had her since she was a chick. My husband and I were stationed overseas when I got her and now, she's my only family since my husband — passed on." She hesitated. "Do you think she'll be all right?"

"I'm sure it's nothing severe. I'll take a fecal and blood sample and then we'll know more. For now, don't worry. I'm sure Bootsie probably just needs a change in diet." I closed up my medical bag. "I'll call you just as soon as I get the results."

The findings showed only slight discrepancies, nothing serious, but what was the life expectancy of a

Taiwanese pheasant? Perhaps Bootsie was only showing aging signs.

I phoned the local zoo. No one there was sure about the longevity of this species. The veterinarian I talked to referred me to another person and another and so on. Finally, I was told to call an individual at the National Zoo in Washington, DC, and, success at last. He was familiar with Taiwanese pheasants and told me that fourteen was "a very old bird indeed."

I now knew how to treat my patient because I was dealing with an aging problem. I altered the bird's nutritional intake and suggested changes to help aging dysfunctions. Bootsie responded and, the last I heard, was doing well.

Although turkeys, ducks or chickens are not uncommon for pets on a farm, in suburbia they are a bit unusual. But more unique than the pet were the circumstances surrounding this case.

Tor, the turkey lived with his two duck companions in a fenced back yard with an adjacent alley, located a level below the owners' house in La Mesa. I was asked to come out on Thursday because Tor had a wound of mysterious origin. I examined the area and was puzzled because there were three puncture-like holes in a triangular formation on his side. Clearly the injury could not have been made by a rogue dog or by his little duck friends or by anything I saw in the yard. What on earth had caused these undefinable marks?

I cleaned the wound and injected Tor with an antibiotic. As I scanned the area still looking for what could have caused the unusual punctures, I noticed that one of the ducks appeared to have an abscess. I mentioned this to the owners who, although they cared about the duck, did not want to spend a lot of money on it. Therefore, I did not take any samples for analysis but simply injected the duck with an antibiotic, too, hoping the drug would help.

At my request, the owners moved Tor to a cage big enough to house a Great Dane that they kept outside the house so that they could keep a closer watch on him. The ducks, on the other hand, were left to roam the fenced yard.

The next night the owners heard quite a commotion in the back yard. They leaped out of bed, hastily put on their robes, grabbed a flashlight and went outside. They checked Tor first — he was fine. Then they went down the hill to the duck enclosure. One duck was missing: the duck with the abscess.

I went back to their house on Saturday. The fence had no holes in it and was too high for an animal to jump over so that ruled out an animal attack. We scratched our heads in wonderment over the situation and then a thought as clear as a Windexed window popped into mind. It had to be the solution to both the attack and abduction because nothing else made sense.

Tomorrow would be Easter.

What better fare for an Easter dinner than a plump turkey! But when that capture failed and the turkey was moved and no longer easily accessible, a duck would do nicely. What a surprise the thief or thieves would have with that particular animal because, after those carefully planned nightly sorties, they had snatched the sickly duck. In its condition, the duck meat would not be tasty as the abscess had undoubtedly tainted the flavor of the entire bird.

Beebee, a four-year-old brown hen, was the family pet since she had been purchased as an Easter chick. Like many chickens raised with love and care, she was a member of the family and included in many of their activities.

I had been summoned to give her a routine physical exam. When I arrived, I called her and she came running, clucking all the way. She looked healthy and her hands-on checkup proved she was in fine condition. I collected fresh droppings for analyzing, just in case there might be an internal parasite.

Being the only pet, Beebee was pampered. For example, she did not have an ordinary chicken coop, she had an extraordinary house. The structure, built like a large doll house, was about six-feet long, four-feet high and four-feet wide. Inside were ramps going up and around and piles of straw to nest in located here and there. The finishing touch to this elegant chicken cottage were the colorful handmade curtains at each window.

In addition to Beebee's private quarters, she had access to the owners' house. They had installed a flap at the bottom of the door so she could go in and out because her food and water were kept in an alcove of the kitchen — a place, of course, specifically for Beebee.

One spring evening, I received a call from a young woman who had been told that I was sympathetic to people who cared for wild animals and she needed my help. June said she was licensed by the California Fish and Game Department to care for wild animals and to help rehabilitate them after they had been injured or because an owner could not keep a full-grown animal.

She had four timber wolves, a black leopard and a mountain lion and, because her current neighbors complained constantly about the animals, she had purchased a ranch in the mountains near Julian with more space and fewer neighbors. Would I be able to help her move the animals to the new location? The cats, she felt, would not be a problem but the wolves would be hard to handle. I agreed to go to her place to assess the situation and see if I could help.

June was waiting for me in back of the house near the animal containment area. All the animals looked in good condition and it was obvious she not only cared for them but took good care of them. Because she had a particularly good rapport with the cats, I thought we could easily get them into containers for transport but the wolves, nervous and fearful by nature, would have to be tranquilized.

June's friend Les volunteered his flatbed truck to move the animals as well as his help in corralling and loading them. We set a date for the relocation.

By the time I arrived, June had everything ready. Les backed his truck with two transport cages on it up to the leopard's area first. He lowered a tailgate ramp that went from the transport cage to the ground level entrance of the existing cage. June, standing in the truck called its name and the leopard, who was quite old and manageable, walked into the new cage as docile as any contented house cat. June secured the gate to its cage.

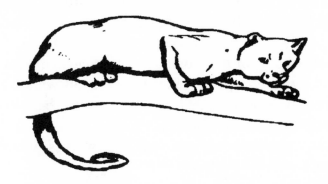

Les maneuvered the truck over to the mountain lion's fenced area. We used the same loading procedure and the mountain lion who obviously adored June, ambled into the new cage without a problem as June murmured soft words of encouragement to it.

We three climbed into the truck and headed towards Julian. I am sure there were a few surprised motorists on that back road also heading towards the mountains when they saw the contents of our load!

In about an hour, we arrived at June's acreage. She had a two-story house nestled among the mountain pines and had made fenced areas for her charges. The holding areas for the wolves had ample ground for running and dog-house-like shelters for them. About ten yards from their area was an approximate twenty- by twenty-foot enclosure for the mountain lion and then about another ten yards from there was a similarly-sized leopard pen.

Les backed up to each enclosure, lowered the ramp and June coaxed the animals into their new homes. The cats sniffed the unfamiliar scents and walked around, exploring the new territory. They appeared interested but did not seem to be upset by the new surroundings.

Phase one of the move was complete and went quite well. June was going to stay here with the cats while Les and I returned to the other house for the wolves. That would be the challenging part of the day.

By the time we arrived, the wolves were very stressed, anxiously pacing back and forth and obviously sensing something was amiss. Les, who had helped June with the wolves frequently in the past, got into the enclosure and singled out a wolf, forcing it over and against the wire fence. Then, I injected the animal with the tranquilizer through the open mesh of the fence.

The animal ran a bit, slowed down to a trot, then a walk and within four or five minutes, lay down peacefully, sound asleep. Because each animal weighed about one hundred-twenty to -thirty pounds, it took both of us to lift and place a wolf in one of the four long thin cages on the truck bed.

This procedure worked fine for three wolves but, number four by now was extremely excited and skittish. Les could not get the wolf over to the fence by simply flailing his arms. He got a four- by four-foot sheet of plywood and used it as a pusher and a restrainer, finally maneuvering the wolf next to the fence where I administered the injection. After the tranquilizer took effect, we moved it into the cage.

Phew! At last we had four nicely slumbering wolves. But there was no time for a congratulatory rest. Les needed to get to the ranch before the sedatives wore off.

June and I decided that it would not be necessary for me to return to the ranch because she knew she and Les could handle the off-loading of the wolves. If there were any problems whatsoever, she had phone numbers where I could be reached and I would return immediately.

I did not hear from her that day so I called the next day, just to satisfy my curiosity. All went smoothly with the wolves, June told me, and the animals seem to be settling in quite nicely.

Over the years, the leopard died of old age and two of the wolves died of heart worms. She has added a bobcat and another wolf and last year was trying to obtain the orphaned cub of a mountain lion that had to be destroyed because it attacked a human.

June and the work she does is most admirable. What is the tragedy is that animals like the ones June tends were purchased or taken from their natural habitat when they were young, in most cases illegally, by people who forgot that the cute little cub will grow into a 200 pound adult with all its wild animal instincts. Its hormones and genetic makeup continually drive it to behave as a wild animal.

It is always sad to see these beautiful creatures condemned to life in a cage because they were raised by humans and, even if they had a chance to be released, they no longer have the animal skills required to survive on their own.

10

Big, Bigger, Enormous

The cartoonist who draws Howard Huge® must have tailored his popular comic strip after seeing this Saint Bernard because Muffin, like Howard, was huge. She was one of the biggest dogs I had ever seen and the largest dog I had ever treated. I estimated she easily weighed 300 pounds, looked the size of a small pony and was big enough that I could sit astride her and my feet would not touch the ground. I said that I "estimated" her weight because no one had a household scale large enough to weigh her and it would be a massive undertaking to get her anywhere that had an adequate scale!

Muffin was about eight years old and having aging difficulties. She had the run of her San Carlos area yard until it was too hard for her to get around and then was confined to the garage. Mary tried to keep her in good condition by exercising her regularly, however, Muffin's physical problems were making exercise almost impossible.

Mary called me out to see if I could help the dog because she seemed to be in a great deal of pain. I examined her as best I could and suspected she had a severe musculoskeletal problem. I felt an x-ray would help pinpoint the dog's problems, but Mary did not want to try to move the dog to an animal hospital so all I could do for the time being was take a blood sample and treat the symptoms.

The results of the test showed some aging dysfunctions and on the basis of that, I prescribed steroids and medications to decrease the pain and to help her arthritic condition. Muffin responded well for about one year then she began to deteriorate rapidly.

When I saw her again, she looked terrible — listless, yelping in pain when we tried to move her and then, when I looked at the mucus membranes of her mouth and at the whites of her eyes, they were yellow, indicating a liver failure.

"The only way we even have a chance of saving Muffin is to get her to a hospital."

Mary looked down. "I don't think so, Doctor. It's gonna be so hard to get her there. Are you sure you can't do something more here?"

I shook my head. "I'm sure you're aware that Muffin's condition is serious. I have done everything I can. She needs to be in a hospital where we can give her tests and continually monitor her condition."

Finally, I convinced Mary that the best for Muffin at this point was to be hospitalized. The date was set and I made all the arrangements at a local, well-known and equipped animal hospital with a staff that included an internist, a board certified surgeon and a highly qualified technical staff.

I arrived at Mary's the next day for the big move. A neighbor had volunteered to drive and let us use his van with large, opening back doors and another male friend of Mary's was there to help. We fashioned a stretcher out of two sturdy long wooden poles with a blanket wrapped around them. Muffin was lying on the floor, too debilitated to walk. We placed the makeshift stretcher alongside the dog's back and all four of us gently rolled her over, on to it.

Now the tough part — moving the dog the ten feet to the van. Each person took one end of a pole and, at the count of "three," we lifted, carried and hoisted our heavy cumbersome load into the truck, huffing and puffing all the way.

While the neighbor was driving Muffin to the hospital, I phoned the staff that the dog would be arriving soon. They were waiting, ready to receive their patient: They maneuvered Muffin onto a gurney and rolled her into the x-ray room.

Unfortunately, the results were not good. The x-ray showed that Muffin had arthritis of the hip and spine and deterioration of the liver and kidneys.

With Mary's permission, we kept Muffin there for a week with little response to medications or treatment. In addition, it was difficult to exercise her properly as she only wanted to lay down which in turn caused bed sores. I felt very helpless and extremely sad when I had to tell Mary that all of us had done everything we could and she was still suffering. I thought the best for Muffin would be to euthanize her.

Two-year-old Fritz was a smaller Saint Bernard, weighing a mere 175 to 200 pounds, who ended up in an unusual predicament. Betty and Dick had called me out to do a routine checkup. The results of the blood test arrived two days later and indicated that Fritz was in good shape and, in addition, Dick had phoned to tell me the dog had no reactions from his vaccinations nor problems with a worming procedure. So, I was a bit surprised when I heard from Betty about two weeks later.

"I don't know what's wrong with Fritz. We take him for a walk and he has fits or seizures or whatever you call them and then he passes out. I have no idea what to do," said Betty.

"Does he have any other symptoms or act like he's ill?"

"No, he seems just fine except when we go walking."

I scratched my chin as I thought. Without actually seeing his symptoms, I really could not come up with any valid ideas about his fainting spells. "I think I'd better come back out and take a closer look at him."

At their house the next day, I romped and played with Fritz while I watched his every movement. I checked him and rechecked him carefully. I simply could not find anything wrong.

"This is most unusual and frankly, I'm puzzled. I can't do or suggest that you do anything until I find out more about these seizures. I want you to write down the time and circumstances when Fritz has a fainting spell. Perhaps that will give me a clue."

Betty called three days later to say Fritz was still fainting almost every time they took him for a walk and would I please come back out. I was there within two hours.

"Well, Fritz, old boy, what's happening?" He wagged his tail and licked my hand.

"Here's the log you asked me to keep." Betty handed me the piece of paper with the times and locations of Fritz's incidents.

As I read them, I thought about Hobie the fainting duck but Fritz's seizures, although similar in that they ended in passing out, were definitely not similar in circumstances. Hobie would faint at the joy of seeing his owners and Fritz was fainting while going for walks with his owners. So, I concluded, perhaps there must be a connection with something they were doing or not doing while walking.

I had an idea. "Could I see the collar and leash you use when you take Fritz for a walk?"

"Sure." Betty walked into the garage and returned with a choke chain collar. She slipped it over his head. "There." Fritz wagged his tail enthusiastically, anticipating the walk that should follow. "Not now, Fritzie. Maybe later." He sat down next to her as if he understood and nudged her with his muzzle.

I looked at the collar. Fritz must be even more uncomfortable in that strangling device than I was when I used to have to wear a necktie. Of course, that must be it!

"Fritz really likes his walks, right?" I asked. Betty nodded. "And I bet he really tugs and pulls on the leash and collar while you're walking." Betty nodded again. "I think the problem is this choke chain that does just that: It chokes him and alters the blood circulation and pressure to the brain which, in turn, causes him to pass out. I think that if you buy him a harness so that the pressure is equally distributed on his chest and abdomen and not around his neck, he'll be just fine."

Betty and Dick had no more fainting problems with Fritz until about one year later. A friend offered to take him for a walk, put on his old choke collar and during the outing, Fritz passed out. This last incident verified that, indeed, the dog's swooning was due to the constriction of his collar. And, if I were forced to wear a necktie again, I might just do the same.

Great Pyrenees originally were used in the Pyrenees mountains to guard sheep and act as guides in this snowy region between France and Spain. They are handsome dogs with long, thick white coats and although they have a formidable stature, weighing between 125 to 150 pounds, I was pleased to discover that my four patients had pleasant dispositions making them easy to examine.

Their owner, Meg Phillips, took excellent care of the two males and two females she owned and, under her management, the animals won many awards in dog shows. Not only were the winning ribbons on display in her house, but so were numerous decorative plates, figurines and attractive bric-a-brac, all picturing her favorite breed, the Great Pyrenees.

Meg called me to come to her house to examine the dogs, give inoculations and most important, to develop a birth control program for the females. She did not want to have them neutered because she eventually intended to breed her dogs with other Great Pyrenees so she wanted a program designed to allow her to control their ovulation. This would make everything from scheduling dog shows to selecting a breeding time much easier.

Birth control pills for dogs are available and effective, I informed Meg, however, there is a risk factor: Some dogs who take the pills develop an inflammation of the uterus, metritis, and if this occurs, the only solution is to spay the dog. Meg felt the risk was worth the reward.

Her dogs had no problems with the pills, Meg continued entering them in shows and a year or so later, she was able to breed them successfully. As far as I know, Meg is still entering her dogs in shows — undoubtedly the offspring of the ones I treated — and I am sure by now the walls of her house are covered and all table tops overflowing with numerous trophies and ribbons.

Pit bulldogs frequently make the headlines because of vicious attacks they have made against people.

Although they have earned a bad reputation, I have not treated any pit bulls with nasty temperaments but I did have one, Spike, with an unusual but not rare condition.

Spike was a blotchy tan and brown dog, weighing thirty to thirty-five pounds with the massive front shoulders common to the species. When he reached sexual maturity he developed paraphimosis, a condition where the penis when extended gets caught outside its sheath and cannot be retracted except while under sedation or, in some cases, anesthesia. The owners brought him to me because he was in extreme discomfort due to this condition.

While Spike was recovering from the anesthetic, I discussed with the owners the necessity of surgery, the only permanent solution to the dog's problem. They were adamant in their negative reply.

However, it did not take long for them to change their minds. About two weeks later and after the third time they had to bring him in, they agreed to his surgery. The procedure went well and the owners had no problems with him after that.

Chow-Chow was — you guessed it — a reddish-brown chow about six months old when Joe, the owner, called me to come to his house, examine the dog and give any necessary inoculations. But, Joe warned, Chow-Chow was definitely hard to manage, was not responding to anyone in the family and, in fact, they were afraid of him. Joe felt I might have problems dealing with him.

"Knowing this," Joe continued, "do you think you would be willing to come out anyway?"

"Of course," I replied while wondering how long it had been since I had been bitten by a dog.

The next day as I packed my medical case, I made sure I had all medications plus a muzzle, just in case. This should be an interesting house call, I thought, as I drove to the south San Diego location.

I parked in front of the house and could see Joe and Chow-Chow waiting for me inside the fenced front yard. "Hi," I called out while opening the gate and entering.

"Let's pretend I'm just a visiting neighbor and sit on these lawn chairs for a while," I suggested. "That way Chow-Chow can get use to me before I examine him."

Joe and I chatted about the dog's general health while I casually dangled my hand over the arm of the chair so that the chow could sniff it. Only a few minutes had elapsed when I felt not only a sniff but an unexpected lick on my hand! I looked down and Chow-Chow was wagging his tail.

"Hi, boy. How are you today?" Much to Joe's amazement, the dog, still wagging his tail, wiggled closer to me and placed his head on my lap, letting his blue-black tongue loll out as he panted. I looked into his friendly brown eyes, patted him on top of his head and scratched him behind his ears.

"Well, I'll be!" Joe exclaimed.

"I guess he likes me," I said, moving from the chair to the porch steps where I could easily reach my medical case. I opened it and began getting out the syringes. Chow-Chow was most curious about what I was doing and, in particular, the open bag must have been irresistibly intriguing because he stuck his nose into it and sniffed vigorously.

Joe was flabbergasted as I gave the dog his exam and shots without so much as a growl from Chow-Chow. "Why can't he be as friendly with us?" Joe asked.

I had no answer. Why is it that an animal can take to one person and dislike others? Is it a scent that a certain person emits, the way words are spoken or maybe it is a way of moving or reacting to an animal? If I knew the answer, I probably could make a fortune by formulating something and selling it to Animal Control officers, veterinarians or others who must deal with unruly animals. No matter what it might be, I was grateful that I had no problems with Chow-Chow.

Few dogs can match a Great Dane for its imposing looks — a massive head, square jaw and a large build, weighing 160 or more pounds. Its ancestors are thought to have been mastiffs and either greyhounds or Irish wolfhounds and although the name Dane indicates an origin in Denmark, they probably originated in Germany.

Because Great Danes are often an inbred breed of dog, they frequently have multiple problems. One complication they share with other large dogs is a susceptibility to stomach twisting. Because they have such large abdominal areas and organs, if the dog jumps or is overly active, the stomach starts to swing and then may twist. When this occurs, there is an immediate toxic response to the system and the dog will soon die if not rushed in for surgery. Danes, as well as other large dogs, also seem to have a great predisposition to respiratory problems with cold-like symptoms.

Val had five or six Great Danes for breeding purposes in her large, fenced back yard adjacent to a canyon area. Because of their size, it was easier for me to make a house call than to have her struggle to bring them in, unless, of course, there was a severe medical problem that required surgery or other treatment that could only be done in the clinic.

With a large number of dogs and the fact that they were large dogs, Val had varied and numerous dilemmas. During the more than ten years I treated her dogs, two of them developed the twisting stomach problem called gastric torsion and although I was able to save one of them, the other one died. According to the pathology findings, another one died of cirrhosis of the liver and atrophy of the adrenal gland. One had arthritic, musculoskeletal problems that I was able to control with medication, another had a problem with ticks that migrated from the canyon area to the dog, while one other had fly bites on the ears that caused infections plus lumps and bumps on the skin that could be controlled but not cured with medication.

One dog had a problem with the valve emptying from the stomach into the intestinal track, the pyloric valve, that could be controlled by nutrition and medicine. Most of her dogs had worms year round because of living in warm southern California so frequent wormings were necessary.

Because she was breeding the dogs, her animals had their share of vaginal and uterine problems that, once again, were controlled with medication. Val was most conscientious and knowledgeable about her dogs and would call me as soon as a problem started so I could act promptly before the unfavorable condition accelerated.

But by far, the most interesting experience I had was with one of her female Danes. This dog, Bonnie, absolutely detested me and would not let me near her. In the past, even giving routine inoculations was impossible for me to do so Val had to be my right and left hand as well as my medical assistant, administering the injections under my supervision.

This time, Val called me out because Bonnie was ready to deliver her pups. I wondered as I drove there if Bonnie would let me touch or help her because she probably was not feeling her usual spunky self.

By the time I arrived, Val had turned her bedroom into a maternity ward for Bonnie. She had moved unnecessary furniture from the room and put her double bed mattress on the floor for the dog to lie on. I peeked into the room and when Bonnie saw me, she lifted her head and growled. That cinched it. There was no way that dog was going to let me near her so Val would once again have to follow my directions and, in this case, be the midwife, a job that fortunately she had successfully done before.

On occasion, I would stick as close to Val as her own shadow when she approached the bedroom doorway so that I could get a quick glimpse of Bonnie without upsetting her too much. However, I spent most of the long night in the living room or at the dining room table, asking questions of Val who was in the bedroom, listening to her replies and then calling out what to do next.

Bonnie started to deliver and Val was by her side, speaking words of encouragement to her. "Here comes number one!" Val called out. "Looks healthy to me." I tiptoed to the doorway and peeked in. Val had already removed the amniotic sac from the puppy's nose so he could breathe and was now cutting the umbilical cord, leaving it about two inches long. She cleaned the puppy with a towel and placed it beside its mother.

I returned to my chair, just as Val said, "Here's number two." I smiled, pleased that the delivery seemed to be going well.

After Bonnie delivered three pups, she acted as though she were finished and as if she wanted to go outside to eliminate. Val escorted her to the door, let the dog out into the front yard and went back to look at the newborns. In a few minutes, Val returned to let Bonnie in. Bonnie walked slowly to the bedroom, stretched out on the mattress and, much to our surprise, delivered another pup!

Unfortunately, this puppy was stillborn. We were saddened by the death but happy that we had at least three puppies —

"Hey, look at this!" Thad, Val's husband, walked into the room from the front yard cuddling a squirming, squealing puppy! Apparently when Bonnie went outside, she had delivered yet another pup. I checked it over and it seemed fine so Val cleaned it up a bit and returned it to its mother, placing it next to the other nursing puppies.

Now the big question was: Had Bonnie delivered all her pups? Because I did not have an x-ray to verify the number of puppies she had carried and I could not touch the dog to feel for other pups and, even if Bonnie would have let me palpate her, the body mass of a Dane is so great that I probably could not have felt any remaining pups anyway. I judged the circumstances of this case, drew from previous experiences and decided that all the puppies had been delivered.

I certainly hoped I was correct because the next step was to give an injection to expel the contents of the uterus.

If I was wrong about the number of puppies and even one puppy remained undelivered, I ran the risk of rupturing the uterus, a serious condition that would require surgery to repair. I filled a syringe, handed it to Val and instructed her where and how to administer it.

I waited an hour to make sure there were no side effects or other problems. All seemed under control so I picked up my medical case and headed out the door.

"Well, not too bad for a night's work, huh?"

"No too bad at all, Doc," Val said, beaming as radiantly as a proud new mother should.

Love Them All

Stray animals come to some people as naturally as fleas to a dog or cat. Usually, these people do not intend to have scores of pets but because of their kind and caring natures, they simply cannot turn down a hungry, homeless animal no matter how many other pets they already have. Some of these animal Samaritans prefer only cats and end up with cat colonies, some are focused on dogs while others simply take in any needy animal, furred or feathered.

With numerous animals come a variety of problems, not only for the owner in stocking enough food and filling water bowls but in keeping inoculations current so that infectious and sometimes fatal diseases will not spread throughout the group. In addition to general housing, if the animal is new to the family and its physical condition unknown or if a pet contracts a contagious disease, quarters to separate the sick from the healthy also must be available.

For the owner, it is easier for the doctor to make one house call than have the owner make many trips to the clinic. For the house call veterinarian there are challenges not found in a clinic atmosphere. With a cat colony, for example, capturing each cat for routine shots or blood tests can be quite an undertaking because the illusive cat can squeeze under, into or behind almost anything. When it is finally captured, another challenge jumps up — making sure the proper cat gets the proper vaccine and the right amount of it. Sounds simple and yet when all-black Blackie looks like coal-black Poker and Poker looks like mid-night-black Inkspot and so on, it is not easy. Because I usually would only see the animals annually, it was diffi-cult if not impossible to see a difference so it was important that the owner, who knew each cat and where it would most likely be hiding, be present to assist in the "hunt and seek" process and make sure I inoculated or treated each animal — and only once.

But even with these minor problems, I enjoyed going to homes with cat colonies because it was a chance to observe the differences between each cat's personality and its response to various situations and conditions. At my arrival, skittish ones would be frightened and streak to some safe hiding place while lazy, napping cats would curiously peer at me through half-opened eyes then return to sleep. A few would casually walk over, sniff my pant legs or shoes then walk away seemingly bored or perhaps self-satisfied with whatever they had detected. On the other hand, the inquisitive ones had their noses in whatever I was trying to do or were wanting to be held and cuddled to the point of slowing down my work by being curious, persistent nuisances.

I have discovered that most neighborhoods have a resident "cat lady," a woman who cannot resist a homeless feline and ends up with many cats. (I never ran across a "cat man" in all of my house call experiences.) If the woman is elderly, frequently she has a fixed, meager income or is living on Social Security and needs help in order to keep her pets healthy. Several organizations are oriented to aid such people and I was a volunteer with one of them, Mercy Crusade. This active group is dedicated to the welfare of small animals and often helps with the costs of care and medication of pets owned by people unable to provide adequately because of limited funds. I believe because of my association as a veterinarian with Mercy Crusade I did more house calls dealing with animal colonies in a year than most veterinarians do in a lifetime.

Sometimes the conditions the owners provided for the animals were as fascinating as the animals themselves. One frail, elderly woman, who could not have properly cared for her pets without the help of Mercy Crusade, had an incredible number of cats confined inside her house — thirty to be precise. As you might imagine, it was difficult to walk anywhere without looking down to make sure you were not stepping on a paw, a tail or a stretched-out body.

With felines outnumbering the human population thirty-to-one, some interior house adjustments were required to make it comfortable for the majority. In addition to the full run of the house, the cats, her "children" as she called them, had two bedrooms devoted to their comfort and pleasure. They had couches, chairs, scratching and climbing posts, numerous play toys and, of course, access to her bed in the corner of one of the rooms. Many food and water bowls were placed throughout the house not only for the convenience of the cat but to try to prevent fights when temperamental FiFi did not want to share a bowl with Felix. Litter boxes, however, were confined to one bedroom and an enclosed porch area near the kitchen.

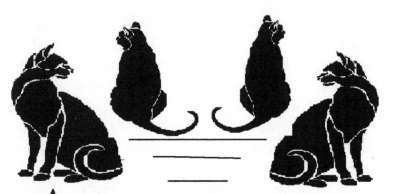

Another woman also with about thirty cats kept the majority of them in two walk-in cages similar to dog runs outside the house while a selected few — about twelve of them — were allowed inside. Although I do not grade people on their living conditions, it is difficult not to observe the surroundings and, in some cases, the diseases or illnesses of the pets can be associated with the areas in which they live. In this woman's house, there was absolutely no cat odor and the floors were so spotless, one could eat dinner off of them. How she managed to keep everything so immaculate I do not know unless she started cleaning in one room, went through the house systematically and then immediately started over.

Of those inside cats, one white kitten with gray spots was unforgettable. Like other kittens, it would jump from the floor to the couch, playfully frolic, leap and casually land upright on all fours. What made this kitten so memorable was that it had no paws, only stubs, because its paws had been cut off accidentally by a lawn mower. Just as so many handicapped pets, it had adjusted quite well and did not seem to recognize it was not like all the other cats.

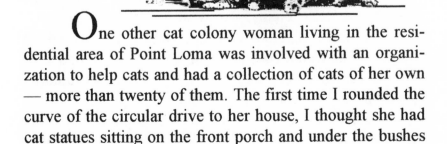

One other cat colony woman living in the residential area of Point Loma was involved with an organization to help cats and had a collection of cats of her own — more than twenty of them. The first time I rounded the curve of the circular drive to her house, I thought she had cat statues sitting on the front porch and under the bushes but a closer look proved the ten or eleven multicolored figurines were alive as they turned their heads or changed positions to better watch my motor home as it approached.

Only a handful were permitted outside, the rest were either in the house or in one of two walk-in cages at the rear of house. Each cat was important to her and she knew where it came from and any idiosyncrasies it might have. On occasion, after thoroughly checking out an individual and deciding he or she was worthy, she would permit the deserving person to adopt one of her cats.

When I first met Lisa, an attractive brunette teacher in her thirties, she lived in a house adjacent to one of the many canyon areas in San Diego where feral cats roam freely. Occasionally, a stray would appear at her back steps wanting a handout or desperately needing medical attention. She would coax and tempt the cat with food until she could catch it. As time went by, the number of captured cats crept up to a plus or minus thirty.

Not only are feral cats hard to capture and often difficult to tame or treat but overall, they are in poor health. Because Lisa, too, was most conscientious about her feline charges, after capturing and before allowing the new cat to be placed with the colony, she would bring it to me for a checkup and blood tests to make sure it had nothing contagious. Of the many cats she brought in, the most common problems were malnutrition, ear mites, eye infections, abscesses, worms, skin problems or a combination of these afflictions.

Dealing with a "wild cat" was not as difficult as it might seem. She would bring it into the clinic in a carrying cage and tell me as much as she knew about the personality of the animal in the brief time she had kept it. The animal in its cage would be placed on the examining table and I would observe it for a few minutes. If the cat seemed relatively calm, I would reach in, place it on the table and soothingly begin running my hands over it, feeling for any noticeable enlargements, bumps or abnormalities while looking for any obvious problems. Then, once the cat was fairly at ease, I could draw blood from the front leg or neck vein with only an occasional minor skirmish. For the truly wild one or two she brought in, I would have to sedate it in order to do any kind of checkup.

If the cat appeared in relatively good condition, she could take it home but had to keep it in isolation until the results of the blood tests came back, usually within twenty-four hours. If the cat was visibly unhealthy or had a wound or condition that needed special treatment, I would keep the cat as long as was necessary.

Because of the numbers of felines needing routine checkups or inoculations, I would go to her house. After she moved from the canyon area to another part of the outskirts of San Diego, the accommodations she made for her cats were outstanding. She enclosed an area down the hill from the house with chicken wire sides and a top that connected to a covered shed. The rustic enclosure had all the amenities that cats love: sofas, chairs, large and small boxes perfect for hiding in, overhead shelves for climbing to, scratching posts, play toys scattered about — you name it, the cats had it!

Although many of the cats looked the same to me, she knew who was who by the creative or descriptive name she had dubbed it. There was Pumpkin, Raisin, Alvin, Andy, Annie, Black Bart, Bert, Blackie, Bootsie, Ernie, Misty, Kalua, Betsy, Mandy, Grayson, Gracie, Poncho, Coco, Hugo, Kit Kat, Minnie, Charley, Willy, T2, Tangelo, Tar, Taro, Amelia, Harry, Mitzi, OJ and CB, short for Orange Juice and Cry Baby and so on.

Most of the cats were kept in the outside pen but whenever a cat tested positive for feline leukemia and could not be kept with the others, it was moved indoors with the rest of her household. In addition to human family members, there were other leukemia positive cats, a bird, hamster, two dachshunds and a German shepherd, a malnourished stray with serious skin problems that she had found and nursed back to good health.

I mentioned the most common ailments the cats had but I did not mention the unusual medical situations that some of them presented. And, it seemed, Lisa more often than not brought in many of my out-of-the-ordinary cases. After so many bizarre instances, it got to the point when she would make an appointment to bring in a stray, I would say to my staff, "Break out the medical books. Here comes Lisa!"

For example, she brought in a cat with a bad case of gingivitis, so bad that when eating, it would gag then vomit. A biopsy of the numerous growths on the gum line around the teeth showed that it had plasma cell stomatitis that produces non-cancerous lesions, possibly associated with an allergic response. Another cat developed a licking problem, probably associated with a psychological disorder. Another had coccidiosis, a protozoan parasite disease that is hard to control. One other cat doubtlessly had received a head injury because, among other problems, one eye pupil never changed size.

By far the most interesting case that Lisa brought in was a female calico she called Mother although the cat had been spayed when it was approximately three years old. I had examined this cat several times in the past and it had no obvious problems, however, when the cat was about ten, Lisa brought her in because she had an enlarged abdomen, was lethargic, not eating well and having trouble breathing. The blood tests showed no viral diseases so I suspected it might be infectious peritonitis. I x-rayed Mother and, to my surprise, discovered a mass in the abdomen that could be a tumor. I decided to do exploratory surgery and what I found was a fairly circumcised oval mass about two and one-half by one and one-half inches adhered to the wall of the abdominal cavity. I removed it and after incising the mass, discovered the hair and bones of a degenerated fetus. She had an ectopic pregnancy before she had been spayed resulting in a mummified fetus. The existing symptoms were surfacing now because she was getting older and having difficulty maintaining the isolation of the mass which was breaking down, releasing toxins into her system and affecting her health.

Mother responded well after surgery and had no problems for about one more year. Then, Lisa brought her in again. After tests, I discovered she had diabetes and several abscessed teeth, both problems possibly caused from the toxic buildup of the previous condition or perhaps just through natural aging. I fixed her teeth and prescribed insulin injections and she recovered quite nicely. Less than a year later, Lisa brought her back and I found she had pancreatitis as well as a polyp under her tongue that I removed plus more bad teeth that I extracted. Once again, she responded well to treatment and the last I heard, she was about thirteen and remaining stable with only insulin.

Ron and Sharon Lewis had an assortment of pets: two dogs, one cat, five birds, two rabbits, a turtle and a hamster. They were constantly concerned about their animals, spent a great deal of time with them and gave them the best of care. With this many and the variety of pets, going to their house or when they would bring a particular animal into the clinic was always a pleasant occurrence because of the numerous adventures or antics they would tell me about their pets.

For example, they trained the first rabbit they got to use a litter box and it stayed in the house until it discovered the delights of chewing telephone cords and electrical wires. They wisely decided this was definitely an unsafe habit and the rabbit must go outdoors so they built a gigantic pen with a mansion-sized hutch for it.

One day the rabbit was let out of its enclosure and got so excited, it hopped lickety-split around the corner of the house, obviously forgot the spa was there, and fell in. Fortunately Sharon was right behind it and pulled out the soaking bunny because it could not have struggled out on its own.

Their talking double yellow-headed Amazon parrot had one of the cleverest responses I ever have heard. When an individual came into the room where it was kept, it would say, "I can talk. Can you fly?"

The indoor hamster loved to explore the house while in its clear plastic ball. We would be sitting in the living room chatting and suddenly, from around the corner, it would roll into the room, tour the area then head out to investigate other quarters.

They volunteered their golden retriever, a breed of dog noted for its friendliness and good disposition, to "work" in a program supervised by Doctor Dennis Fetco, an animal behavioral psychologist. Their dog as well as other pets were taken to local children's hospitals to help boost the children's spirits. Of course, any animal in this program needs to be well trained and mind commands but the main "work" it does is to allow the children to pet and love it.

Their other dog, a Doberman pinscher, had a puzzling problem. The Lewis' brought her in because she had developed an unusual swollen area in the middle of her back that looked suspiciously as though it might be a tumor. I decided to surgically re-

move the Vienna-sausage-sized growth and sent it to the laboratory for pathologic analysis. Was I surprised when the results showed that its core was composed of plant material and when I saw it, it looked a bit like cactus spines.

I called the Lewis' with the news and asked about the dog's routine. They said the dog was walked twice a day and loved to sniff in and under the bushes and trees. I suspected that it had brushed against something with cactus-like spines, the spines had penetrated the skin and its body had walled off the foreign matter, eventually causing the visible growth.

Then, about a month later, at the end of the incision line where the mass had been removed, another mass began to grow. I removed it and again, the laboratory results showed it was composed of the same material as the first.

I called the Lewis' and Sharon said the dog had not been outside on its usual walks. Therefore, this could not be a new condition so it had to be a continuation of the previous one. Probably the elusive material had migrated and any that I had not removed during the original surgery showed up later.

During the next six months, I surgically removed four more similar masses. I still am not certain why it took so long for some of the spines to fester and cause the tissue reaction but I suspect it had to do with where they were located on the dog's back — the higher area, over the center of back, where it received more trauma from rubbing than the lower areas. It has been at least four years since the last operation so I believe all the troublesome spines are finally gone.

The Lewis' would let me borrow their white Moluccan cockatoo Doc, my namesake, when I needed a live prop for a media interview. In general, he behaved well and seemed to enjoy the attention. Four, maybe five years after I last had taken him out, Sharon called to say that Doc was acting belligerent towards her, was difficult to handle and biting her finger hard but not hard enough to draw blood. She asked why he was doing this and what could she do to stop it. I inquired about the circumstances sur-rounding these occurrences — when did they happen, who was there or not there or any other pertinent details. After analyzing what she told me, I decided that Doc, a male bird, did these undesirable behaviors when her husband was near so probably the bird was jealous. I suggested that whenever he acted this way, to banish him to his cage, cover the cage for about ten minutes, then bring him back out. This procedure worked for four or five more years until a serious mishap took place.

Doc was acting mean and aggressive so Sharon put him in his cage and covered it. After a short time she returned to see if he had calmed down and was less antagonistic. As she put her face close to the bars of the cage to talk to him, he reached through the bars, grabbed her lower lip and severely ripped through it, tearing out a chunk of flesh. Ron was at home, heard her screams and rushed her to the emergency room of the hospital. The doctor sutured the wound but everyone realized that because of the severity of this laceration, plastic surgery would be required to rebuild and restore her lip tissue. Although it was a long drawn out series of operations, I am happy to report that if a person did not know what had happened, one would never realize the accident had occurred.

As far as what happened to Doc — Ron was, as you might guess, beside himself with anger and afraid for Sharon's safety. If a horrible thing like this happened once, it could happen again. He called me, wanting to have the bird euthanized so it would never hurt anyone again. I talked him into giving the bird to me until I could find another home for it. Fortunately, one of my staff at the clinic, a bird breeder, was willing to take Doc. The latest news from her, about three years after this awful incident, was that the bird was doing well and she had no problems with him. Possibly he was adjusting because he has a female cockatoo partner.

Unfortunately, Doc was not unique in his aggressive behavior. All varieties of cockatoos are notorious for biting, injuring and sometimes even killing their mates during mating season. And, the larger the species of cockatoo, such as the Moluccan, the more dangerous. The precise cause of these attacks is unknown but they occur most often in the early part of the breeding season. Perhaps the cockatoo hen's failure to respond to a soliciting male may facilitate an attack although attacks have happened in breeding pairs even after years of a stable productive relationship.

Although many owners of cockatoos rarely have a problem, owners of male cockatoos should be alert to aggressive behavioral changes and take precautions to prevent harmful encounters. Some of these signs are territorial aggression, nest building, courtship attitudes and attempted copulation even toward a human. In the case of Doc and Sharon, in all probability the bird, now a mature male, was reacting to Sharon as though she were his mate, a mate who had shunned his advances by putting him in a cage. In retaliation, he did what came instinctively to a cockatoo. Although most attacks occur between a male cockatoo and a human female, a man also should be aware and alert because he may be perceived as a competitor and therefore subject to attack.

Another family, the Madisons, had four cats and soon acquired four puppies, pups that when mature, they hoped to breed and then to sell the offspring. Unfortunately, when selecting the animals, they let the cute, irresistible qualities of each sway them — their emotions ruled their choices — and they took the pup home without taking the necessary basic steps.

First, they should have checked with the breeder regarding the previous breeding record or the parentage of the animal and, second, if all records seemed appropriate, taken the animal to their veterinarian for a thorough physical before finalizing the purchase. Although neither checking lineage nor having a physical checkup for the pet is an absolute guarantee that the animal will be an ideal breeder, it certainly might uncover some possible future problems. If they had done these two steps before taking the animal home and making it a member of the family, they might have avoided the scenario that ensued.

One Samoyed they purchased developed an infection of the uterus, a condition that could not have been foreseen and, unfortunately, that could only be corrected by spaying. However, after surgery, she had problems with bleeding that indicated a coagulation syndrome, an inability for blood to coagulate properly that is often an inherited trait. In addition, she developed a hip disorder that causes lameness. It, too, is an inherited condition and, even if she had not been spayed, it would be inadvisable for her to have pups because this is considered a genetic defect.

The other Samoyed, although appearing physically healthy, developed multiple allergies that resulted in itching, swellings, hives, sneezing and loss of hair. Its sensitivities to these various allergens were controllable with medication, however, she inherited these allergies and could pass them on to her pups genetically. It was not advisable to breed her.

They next bought a toy Maltese male and, after observing it for a few days, felt that something was wrong or unusual about the dog and brought it to me for a checkup. A quick examination revealed that it had an incompletely closed urethra that made it resemble a vulva and smaller than normal testicles. I had run across a similar situation previously and knew that this, too, was a case where a hormonal imbalance occurs during development in the uterus resulting in an incomplete male, a pseudohermaphrodite. Although surgery might correct the visible deformities and the dog might be able to breed, not only would costs for the operation be exorbitant but I felt breeding was not wise because this was probably a genetically transmitted condition. Once again, they had another dog that they should not breed.

All dogs have a nictitating membrane in each eye, a third eyelid or membrane with glands that sometimes must be surgically removed because it becomes infected or injured. The removal of this membrane in their Lhasa Apso would not affect any breeding plans they might have for her but, the umbilical hernia that required surgery to repair suggested they should not breed her because this condition does have a genetic predisposition. Their batting average of zero for four was most disappointing.

The dogs by now were too much a part of the family to return or to sell. Although their major plan to breed dogs came to a screeching standstill, they did end up with delightful pets.

If you are not buying an animal for breeding or show purposes, the lineage of it probably is not important. But the wise potential owner of any animal should insist that it be taken to a veterinarian for a complete checkup before taking it home. If something is wrong with the animal, the buyer then has the relatively unemotional choice of whether to keep the pet and deal with its probable future problems or to look for a more appropriate animal. Because, once that new fluffy kitten or bouncy dog is brought home, it soon snuggles its way not only into your arms but your heart. It becomes an important part of your life, a part that is most difficult to give up.

Military

Assignments

Marine Mammals

If someone had told me when I was a student at Michigan State University focusing on the care and treatment of small animals that eventually I would be a veterinarian in charge of marine mammals, I would have laughed and said, "You've got to be kidding!" I also would have been amused if someone informed me that when I joined the Air Force in 1958, in 1977 I would be a part of the US Navy. Yet, this unforeseeable combination happened.

The Navy did not have a veterinarian qualified for this assignment and I was available and, even though at that time I wondered how truly qualified I was for the job, I accepted it. I would be responsible for the medical care and supervision of marine mammals at three different locations in San Diego and the senior veterinarian for those kept at military bases in Hawaii.

What a change this new job and its location would be! I was leaving my Washington, DC area office and the bustling, people-filled Pentagon surrounded by the noises of a big city to join a staff of about a dozen in a mobile trailer office near the end of Point Loma, a rock's toss from the ocean where the loudest noises would be the pounding surf on the coastal cliffs. Indeed, I was delighted to trade my fluorescent light indoor pallor for a healthy southern California outdoor glow and looked forward to the challenges that awaited me.

For the first time in my life, I would get to work with and study marine mammals, fascinating creatures that had always intrigued me. Any information I and my staff gathered, regarding the physiology, psychology, behavioral patterns and ecologies of the various species would be shared, both nationally and worldwide, with civilian institutions and universities including organizations such as the International Association for Aquatic Animal Medicine. At no time would the studies of these mammals be harmful to them.

Within a month, I was in my new surroundings, getting acquainted with the staff, the fully-equipped diagnostic laboratory and my marine mammal charges. The staff included another Air Force veterinarian, two US Navy SEAL team medical corpsmen, Doctor Sam Ridgway the chief of the Marine Biological Science Division and three of his staff plus a secretarial crew of three.

The pens and tanks for the marine mammals could accommodate a total of eighteen and generally we had a full house. In each of the eight pens, we could care for one marine animal that does not need to be wet all the time such as a fur seal, harbor seal or California sea lion because these species usually are not compatible in close quarters. Each twelve- by four-foot wide cement pen had a shelter, slides, an almost square three-foot deep water trough and a door that opened onto a common area with a pool about ten- by fifteen-feet and eight-feet deep. Around the pool were elevated platforms for sunning.

Unlike sea lions, Atlantic bottlenosed dolphins are social animals that need companionship so usually three dolphins could be kept in each of the two twenty-foot in diameter by six-foot deep circular tanks and up to four dolphins in the twelve-foot deep tank. These reinforced fiberglass tanks, on the compound before our project began, were designed to store the fresh water from a desalinization plant, one of the first sea to fresh water conversion plants ever constructed in the States. However, during the Cuban missile crisis in the 1960s, because Castro shut off the water supply to the US Navy base at Guantanamo, our government dismantled and shipped the plant, but not the water storage tanks, to Cuba where they were needed.

The tanks had remained unused until we filled them with recirculating sea water, pumped from the ocean, filtered before entering the enclosures and tested daily for pollution and potentially infective organisms. This was a highly sophisticated, well-monitored water system that met the animals' requirements and, before pumping the water back into the ocean, it was further treated to meet environmental safety standards.

Most of the marine animals under my care at this seaside compound were here because they were sick, injured, had been captured accidentally by fishermen or were given to us by an aquatic park that could not properly care for them. They were animals that could die if left in the wild without lifesaving medical treatment or care.

Each animal was examined at least once a week and if just an oral medication was required, giving it to the patient was easy. The drug plus a vitamin and mineral supplement and a heart worm pill in the case of a sea lion were slipped inside a mackerel, squid, herring or smelt, depending upon which fish was nutritionally the best for that species, and hand-fed to the animal.

Most of the dolphins were the slate to bluish gray Atlantic bottlenosed dolphins, seven- to ten-feet long and were easier to tame, train and medically treat than the occasional gray Pacific bottlenosed dolphin we would get. This dolphin weighed more and was more aggressive and difficult to handle, particularly, when it had to be moved out of the water for tests or medication.

When we had to move any dolphin to land, I and my four or five man crew had a well-organized plan, worked quickly and competently to gather the necessary information, administer the medication if necessary and return the animal to the water within forty minutes or less. The shorter the time, the better for the animal, not because it was out of water, but because of the stress created by moving it to land. This stress could cause a previous condition to flare up or bring on a kidney or liver dysfunction that would not appear during the next day or week but could surface months later and could cause permanent damage to these organs.

The first step in the catching process was to lower the water level in the tank to a depth so that the animal could still float and we could maneuver easily — about two-feet deep or calf high for us. All those needed for the capture, generally a minimum of three, in wet suits, entered the tank and stretched a net across one section of it. They slowly moved forward, edging the desired dolphin away from any others in the tank and when close enough, one man would grab the dolphin around its body, in front of its dorsal fin while the other net holders would close the net around it.

Although corralling may sound easy it is not always a simple task and can be dangerous. As the dolphin races towards its captor with teeth bared and looking most fearsome, it then changes tacks, swings around and with its strong tail, hits the person in the knees with enough force to knock down a 200-pound man caught off guard. One SEAL medic was hit so hard by the tail of Ivan the Terrible, a Pacific dolphin named for his nasty disposition, that his knee cap was shattered and the surrounding ligaments ruptured so badly that he retired on medical disability about four months after the accident.

Once the dolphin was in the net, the men had to make sure to lay back the flippers because they could be broken, just like a person's arm. The next step was to move the netted dolphin onto a stretcher for lifting ashore. Usually, it was the job of the corpsman, a well-trained SEAL team medic, to grab the dolphin with a bear hug around the midsection and head it towards the stretcher.

The stretcher was made of two seven-foot-long aluminum poles with a nylon and plastic reinforced canvas between them, frequently with a sheepskin insert over the canvas to prevent scratches to the animal's skin. As soon as the dolphin was on the stretcher, the net had to be removed carefully because if not done right, the dolphin could flip out of the stretcher, back into the water and the whole catching procedure would have to begin again.

Once on the stretcher, the dolphin was raised by a lifting hoist with weighing scale attached to determine its actual weight, somewhere between 800 and 1,000 pounds, and then hoisted out of the tank by a crane. It was then lowered onto a skin-protecting rubber mat, placed on the ground adjacent to the tank. At this point, the roundup time was anywhere from fifteen minutes to a full hour.

The next challenge was to keep it from hurting itself because, like a fish out of water, when frightened, it flops vigorously. Dolphins are extremely powerful and when they flex, they do so with an enormous force at the tail and head area. The strongest members of our crew were always positioned at these areas because by simply throwing their body weight on the tail or head while wrapping their arms around the dolphin, they could generally restrain most of the animal's movement. On occasion, however, even hefty men can not hold a determined dolphin.

We had successfully lowered Pandora, an Atlantic bottlenosed dolphin, to the mat and five of us pounced on her along her backside. A 230-pound man lay across the head section, a 250-pound male was on the tail, and a 210-pound and 180-pound man were on the inside edge of them and I, at 190 pounds, was at the midsection. A female laboratory technician was kneeling on the stomach side of the animal ready to take a vaginal smear because we wanted to learn more about breeding or vaginal infections.

She pointed to the area and asked me, "Right about here, Doctor?" She gently touched the vagina with the swab.

With that, this usually docile dolphin, flexed then flopped in a fish-like motion moving about eight feet forward, catching all of us off guard and tossing off everyone but me whom she dragged along with her. Quickly the men regained their balance, came to my rescue, pinned down the dolphin and, by rotating her gently, moved the mat back under her. Fortunately, no one was hurt except me: I had skinned knees because I was wearing shorts.

"This time, wait until I tell you we're ready," I said to the technician who was looking a bit frightened and most apprehensive.

We held fast to the dolphin with renewed strength and determination. "All set?" I asked.

"Yes," each replied.

"Okay. Try it again."

She used the eight-inch standard culturette and within seconds the smear was accomplished. The dolphin was returned to the stretcher, a blood sample taken and she was lifted and lowered into the tank. The SEAL team medic stayed in the tank for about ten minutes to watch for any signs of discomfort in the animal. None was noted, the tank was refilled and during the next eight to ten hours, the dolphin was observed for any abnormal signs.

Perhaps the most loved and showered with attention marine mammal we ever cared for was a baby California sea lion. The pregnant mother had washed ashore and a few days after being given to us, she bore her pup.  Two days later, the mother died from internal parasites and pneumonia and the pup was ours to hand raise. Liberty became a group project for the veterinarians and biological staff.

We devised our own formula for him by taking ingredients and proportions from mixtures created by other marine mammal specialists attempting to raise orphaned pinnipeds. Our recipe started with twenty scaled herring whose heads, dorsal, pelvic and pectoral fins were removed. The fish were then sectioned, placed in a blender along with vitamins, minerals and a sugar solution and mixed thoroughly.

Liberty had to be fed our special mixture every four to six hours except from 10 p.m. until 6 a.m. when the facility was closed. We all took turns with this time-consuming feeding assignment that, by itself, could be considered a full time job. He was bottle-fed for two weeks until his teeth became so sharp that he would bite through the bottle's nipple. We had to switch to a tube with syringe that was an effective way to get the formula down but a messy procedure for us because he would spit it out over our arms and clothing like a baby being burped. Evidentially, in spite of all the spilled formula, he got enough to eat and it must have been nutritious because Liberty gained weight rapidly.

After he was weaned, Liberty received a privilege the other animals did not: He often was allowed out of his cage to roam the compound. Although not considered dangerous, he did pose a threat to anyone assigned to the feeding team who did not keep a watchful eye on him. As the person approached a cage, he or she would set down the two buckets filled with fish in order to open the door and, as quick as a blink of the eye, Liberty would knock the buckets over and gobble up all the fish before the feeder could stop him. On occasion, he would even sneak up behind an unwary person and brazenly knock the bucket out of his hand to get the fish.

Liberty became a strong, healthy, handsome and most vocal sea lion. When he was old enough, he left us to be trained as part of the SEAL team. The last I heard, he is still in San Diego, loved by everyone who works with him and seems quite content to be with humans, undoubtedly, because he has always been around them.

When ailing pinnipeds in our compound were well, we returned them to the ocean. Generally, the animals were set free one at a time, however, this day we had three healthy California sea lions ready to leave and decided to turn the trio loose as a group, wondering what direction each would take. We put them in individual cages, carried them to the water north of our office, let them loose and yelled good-byes as they swam off.

We watched as one of them went straight out to sea and was not seen again by us. One headed south, rounded Point Loma and two days later climbed onto a docked submarine on the bay side where the startled sailors called us to come and get him. The third sea lion apparently knowing he had found "the good life" had swum south far enough to clear the fence, crawled up the embankment and was waiting for us when we returned to the compound, barking to be fed.

He stayed with us until he grew to such enormous proportions we could not accommodate him and the San

Diego Zoo offered to take him. Zoo officials commented that he was one of the biggest sea lions they had ever seen and the truck that hauled him to his new home must have agreed because it moaned pitifully with the weight of the sea lion as it slowly climbed the hill.

In addition to our pens and tanks on the ocean side of Point Loma, the bay side of the point and Coronado had open-water wire enclosed pens for sea lions and dolphins. Here the mammals were tamed and trained by SEAL volunteers who were willing to accept a long-term commitment to work with them, knowing that it was a twenty-four-hour a day job, whether on or off duty. Each trainer had a beeper so that he could be notified and return immediately if something were wrong with his animal and, generally, something was always happening. These men were deeply devoted to their charges and the bond between the trainer and his assigned mammal was as strong as that between a boy and his dog. Frequently, because of this close relationship, only the trainer could handle the animal successfully so, if the marine mammal was assigned duty in another locale, the trainer accompanied his animal.

I and my corpsman always went to the particular facility to treat or examine a sick dolphin because it was easier for us to travel to the dolphin than to transport it to us because it had to be kept in water or wet. The sea lions were easier to move so often an ailing one was brought to us.

At least twice a year when complete physicals were needed for the sea lions, they were put in transport cages, loaded in a truck and brought to us. Even if we had not been notified they were coming we would have known they were arriving because, as the vehicle came down the steep hill to the compound, we could hear them, barking like banshees all the way. At this time blood and fecal samples were taken, an examination of the ears and, if possible, the mouth were done. If the animal was in an unpleasant mood, it was impossible to look into a mouth without getting severely bitten. Getting a blood sample from a sea lion is not easy either: The syringe needs to penetrate the skin in the spinal area where blood vessels are accessible but hard to locate because they are far below the skin. Sometimes I would try unsuccessfully two or three times to draw blood, turn to other examining procedures, then try again, eventually accomplishing the task.

Most of the marine mammals being trained in the San Diego area were sea lions, although there were two or three Atlantic bottlenosed dolphins in training. All were trained and exercised in open water to retain their proficiency in the search and rescue of men, to find lost objects or locate small munitions, bombs, torpedoes, sunken ships or downed aircraft on the bottom of the ocean.

During one dolphin training session in San Diego bay, a SEAL team was also practicing maneuvers — tactics that had an unexpected finale. The men were to be dropped from a transport aircraft into the waters south of the Coronado bridge and then would be retrieved by aircraft. The first man jumped, landed in the water and was treading water while waiting to be picked up when he felt a nudge on his back. He told me later his heart jumped into his throat because he thought that he was being attacked by a shark. He looked fearfully behind him — and there was the playful dolphin. As the remaining six SEAL members hit the water, each was thumped in the back by the dolphin and each thought instantly, "Shark!" Later that afternoon, in no uncertain terms, the SEAL team informed the dolphin trainers to "Keep your animals locked up during our exercises and NEVER let them do that again."

When winter storms lashed the coast, we could count on receiving numerous calls from people who had found a weather-torn animal beached or stranded on the rocks and needing medical attention. We would capture the animal with a net, put it in a vehicle we had equipped with medical supplies and items necessary for capture and move it to our facility. We cared for the animal until it regained its health; if it could fend for itself, it would be released; if not, and we did not have a vacant pen, we would arrange for it to be transferred to another place such as Sea World or the San Diego Zoo. It was not unusual to acquire half a dozen new patients during the stormy season. Although we were not required to care for these animals — it was not part of our duties — any animal in need of help was taken in when we had the space. All personnel, especially eager corpsmen and technicians, volunteered their time.

After one bad storm, three common dolphins, indigenous to the California coast, washed up on the beach, we rescued them and placed them in the big tank. In a few days when they started feeling better, they began jumping with leaps so high we had great concern that they might accidentally land out of the tank. They never did and the only conclusion we could make regarding these extraordinary leaps was the dolphins were jumping to see how far it was back to the ocean.

During another storm, a staff member spotted a gray harbor seal washed ashore near our compound. We donned our foul weather gear, netted him, put him on a stretcher, carried him back and put him into an empty sea lion cage. For the next two weeks, we took turns doctoring, feeding and caring for him and in three months time, he was healthy and ready to leave and would be shipped to San Clemente Island to be released. When the time came to say good-bye, all of us were sad because he was such an easy animal to treat, so friendly and genteel, that we would miss him.

Of all the animals I treated that surprised me the most because of their delightful ways were the two Beluga whales. The Navy brought them from the Arctic to the enclosures at bay side to determine if they would be suitable for training and use in cold waters where dolphins and sea lions would not work. Each weighed about eight hundred pounds and was about thirteen feet long, they were, in my opinion, the "cutest" of our marine family. To touch their light ivory colored body was like feeling putty or soft clay and to work with them was easy because they were so docile that all medical treatment could be done in the water. They enjoyed having their heads rubbed and seemed to like the company of people so much that they would swim along, following anyone who strolled the walks that went around the tanks.

Their trainers routinely informed me about the whales' physical conditions or if any unusual symptoms or characteristics developed that might signal a physical problem. They also told me they were making some progress in training them, however, by the time my assignment at the compound ended, it was too soon to tell if the program would be successful.

Unlike the harbor seal that we hated to see leave and the lovable Beluga whales, no one would regret the departure of the four-foot Alaskan fur seal, found ill in the Bering Straits and sent to us for treatment. Also known as the Pribolof or northern seal, this species is well-known for its territorial ways, viciousness and hostility towards man and it lived up to its reputation.

One would think that because she was extremely sick, she would be too weak to fight but this was not the case. From the first time we examined her, discovering that in addition to serious medical problems and parasites, she was pregnant, to the last time we did a routine check on her, she fought us making each session a grueling, lengthy and dangerous battle. Once the capture net was around her, she growled, thrashed about and tried to bite anyone within reach. Heavy gloves were mandatory when working with her and I could examine her only after one of the assistants grabbed her around the neck to keep her from turning her head back to bite me. Because she was so bad tempered, we could not remove the net so I had to examine her through its openings.

The pup was born in poor condition two weeks after her arrival and, although we tried desperately to save it, it died three days later. During those few days, however, we all learned something: A baby fur seal makes a sound like the bleat of a lamb.

Because this mature seal was already here and little was known about training this species, another veterinarian and technician volunteered to attempt to tame and train her. The training went slowly and was most difficult because the seal fought them as determinedly as it had us. The last I heard, the idea of trying to tame or train fur seals was abandoned because they were too unpredictable and the job too time consuming. The seal was given to the Department of Fish and Game to return to its natural environment.

The two years I spent on loan to the Navy was truly a learning experience. Not only did I increase my knowledge about aquatic mammals but my admiration deepened for these sometimes cantankerous, but most of the time, lovable creatures.

13

Island Adventures

Special assignments occasionally took me to places where accommodations or conditions were not always up to the standards of a one star hotel, let alone a four star one. One time, I flew to the Gulf of Mexico to oversee the care of six Atlantic bottlenosed dolphins during a twenty-hour air transport maneuver. The marine mammals were quite comfortable in their wet berths and with the chilly temperature inside the cargo plane. On the other hand, I sat in an uncomfortable jump seat, shivering constantly and was totally miserable during the entire sleepless flight.

Another trip where I would be "roughing" it occurred in May, 1978, when I traveled to San Miguel Island,
one of the Channel Islands, off the coast of California. San
Miguel, about seven and one-half miles long with a width
of two to three miles, is owned by the Navy, administered
by the Channel Island National Park and is a breeding area
and rookery for sea lions and considered the southern most
habitat for the northern fur seal. The serious purpose of this
duty was to gather information that might indicate why sea
lion pups were being born prematurely or dying shortly
after birth. Previous research indicated the cause might be
one of four conditions: One, leptospirosis, a spirochete
disease that is contagious and deadly; two, some type of
unique virus; three, a parasitic condition; or, four, environmental contaminants. It was hoped that continuing
research could pinpoint the problem and lead to a solution.

I and Mary Platter-Rieger who worked with me flew
to Santa Barbara by commercial aircraft, then switched to a
chartered four-seat Cessna that landed on the dirt airstrip
near the center of the island. We off-loaded our gear and
waved farewell to the pilot. I breathed deeply, filling my
lungs with the fresh damp sea air. The afternoon sun
warmed my face and I looked up at the blue sky splashed
with fleecy clouds and carefree gulls making lazy spirals. It
was an ideal day for a walk and I was anxious to get
moving, to explore an island I had never seen and one that
few people outside of scientific and research personnel see
because, no one without a permit is allowed access to its
interior.

"All set?"

Mary nodded, pushed her glasses higher on her nose and replied, "Let's go."

We hoisted our backpacks loaded with personal gear and each of us grabbed a handle of the ice chest, filled with dry ice and medical equipment necessary for taking samples. Low, dry grass and green shrub-like vegetation covered the ground as far as I could see except on the only trail, a nearly flat dirt path that wound northwesterly towards the area that would be home for the next six days.

In about forty minutes, I was huffing with the weight of the load and the length of the hike and glanced over to see how Mary was holding up. Although I outweighed her by about seventy pounds, towered above her by a good ten inches, thought I was in good shape and was only a mere ten years older, obviously, she was in far better condition than I because she did not seem the least bit weary.

"How are you doing?" I asked, hoping she would like to rest for a few minutes.

"Fine. We'll soon be there. In fact, I think I see the cabin in the distance."

I squinted in the direction she was looking and thought I saw a roof top, too. "Great! This is quite a hike. Must be a good six miles from the landing strip to the cabin."

Mary laughed and smoothed her wind-ruffled brown hair with her free hand. "You're joking. It can't possibly be more than three miles."

With a sheepish grin, I said, "Sure, just kidding," and thought: Time to start jogging and exercising more as soon as I get home.

We arrived at the house, sat down the gear and, although we would sleep outside in individual tents, not in the cabin, knocked on the door to inform the almost full-time residents on the island, we were here. Bud Antonellis and his wife, also specialists in the scientific research field, welcomed us into their rustic, frequently shared home. The modest interior contained beds for them and their two children, additional single beds for visiting scientists or researchers, a kitchen with propane stove, a refrigerator, a dining table and chairs, a radio and, through the window, I could see the nearby outhouse. It definitely was not the Hilton but it was cozy and livable.

Bud briefed us on the basics: Meals would be prepared in the kitchen for them, us and the two other researchers already on the island by whomever volunteered to cook that day. Dishes were done on a volunteer basis also. Breakfast would be at about eight o'clock, sack lunches would be available to take to the work site and dinner would be at six.

"If you want to take a shower or a bath — " he smiled, " — yes, we even have a bathtub," Bud opened the door and pointed, "that's the trail you take. It's about a mile away with cold but invigorating spring water and outside bathing. There are so few of us on the island, it still can be private if you just make it known you're going there.

"The other trail leads to the laboratory that's about a half mile from here. Although you can't see it from the lab because of a hill, the beach is only about 200 yards away."

"The lab," I looked at Mary. "We just have time to take the cooler there and see what it's like before dark."

"Let's go."

We thanked Bud, picked up the chest between us again and headed down the foot path. Unlike the trail to the cabin, this winding path went up and down several small hills sprinkled with yellow and white flowering plants growing close to the ground. I spotted and could identify numerous island mallow plants by their large palmate leaf and pink blossoms and the shrub-like coreopsis with its distinctive feathery leaf.

A spur from the main trail ended at the doorway of the lab, a six- by three-foot wooden building that looked more like a shed than a science laboratory. Inside were a narrow, waist-high work bench that ran almost the length of it, a Bunsen burner, trays, a microscope, vials, saws, knives and miscellaneous other surgical instruments. Like the cabin, it was rudimentary but adequate.

"Seen enough for now?" I asked.

"Yes. Let's head back and set up our tents."

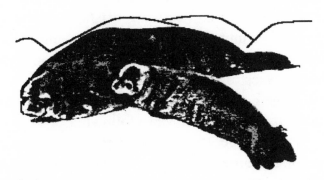

After breakfast the next day, Mary and I stuffed our lunch sacks in our backpacks and headed first to the laboratory where we left the packs and then to the hilly trail towards the beach. We reached a knoll and caught our first glimpse of the beach where hundreds of marine mammals splotched the sand. Although we were too far away to do a precise count or to see how many were sick or dead, we could identify numerous sea lions, both adults and pups, and a few gray elephant seals, basking in the sun. I led the way, trudging down the hill and then up to the top of the last obstacle, a sand dune. Without thinking, I popped up over its crest and immediately the animals, startled by my jack-in-the-box arrival, dashed into the ocean, barking loud warnings of displeasure at being disturbed.

"Well, I learned something," I shouted over the din. "If you want to observe them, sneak up to the top of this dune."

Although we knew what we would find due to our assignment, actually seeing the panorama as it was now saddened us. All the animals that were healthy or well enough to move were swimming offshore. The dozen or more remaining animals were sea lion pups, either awash in the surf line or near death on the beach or already dead and in varying stages of decomposition.

I sighed. "Let's get to it," and headed down the dune, onto the beach with Mary following.

The schedule started that day would be my work routine for the duration of my stay. For the most part, I would be working alone although Mary helped me with laboratory duties whenever necessary. When not busy with their assignments, the other researchers brought me the

necessary specimens which was greatly appreciated because the most exhausting part of my assignment was
getting carcasses to the laboratory. Each weighed about
twenty-five pounds, a heavy and awkward load to carry or
drag up and over the hill to the shed. Once placed on the
work table, I did a necropsy, and took tissue and organ
samples that I placed in jars numbered to correspond to the
number the dead animal was given. These jars were then
packed around the dry ice in the cooler and would be taken
to San Diego for further studies and tests after Mary and I
left the island. For each carcass, I made a detailed report
that included the length, weight, condition of the body or if
it had missing parts, bruises or other obvious abrasions.

Whenever I had free time during the day, I explored
the island and observed the wildlife. On a hike to the bluff
above the beach, I found nests of Western gulls made of
straw-like grass and each with two or three duck-sized dark
brown eggs in them. As I strolled the beach, the lolling sea
lions with grumbling barks, would leave the beach ahead of
me, and like a great gray wave, return to it behind me.

On one sandy walk, I saw more than a two thousand
pound, dark gray elephant seal sprawled on the beach.
These are the largest pinnipeds with males weighing up to
four tons and, to me, are peculiar looking because of their
long trunks or snouts that can be pushed out into a bladder
and used possibly to frighten enemies.

I had never seen one up close and because he did not
appear to be breathing, I decided to move nearer. I walked
over, cautiously circled around him and still he did not

move. Certainly, if he were alive, he would have been bothered by my presence and fled so, I concluded, he must be dead. I started to push him with my hands, hoping to roll him over enough to discover what might have killed him. With that shove, he lifted his head, let loose

a boisterous trumpeting snort and looked straight at me while righting himself. My heart raced as fast as an entry in the Grand Prix and I jumped back and ran inland as quickly as I could in the loose sand, looking over my shoulder to see if this marine behemoth was following. He, apparently as frightened as I, moved amazingly fast towards the water looking like an enormous caterpillar too fat to lift its stomach off the ground, whose insides seemed to move first with its rippling skin following.

Every night after dinner when each finished his or her necessary paperwork, we shared our daily findings that included anything from a minor description of a colorful flower to the playful antics of the sea lions or to more unusual sightings. One researcher saw a Stellar sea lion on the small island in the cove, a very exciting discovery to everybody because these spotty gray animals, twice as big as the California sea lion and the largest member of the sea lion family, are rarely found this far south. Mary whose hobby is ornithology was thrilled with her sighting of a red-billed tropic bird, a bird that lives primarily in Hawaii and also is rarely seen here.

The island was also home to ground squirrels, other rodents and the gray Channel Island fox, a subspecies of the mainland gray fox, about the size of a house cat. All any of us had to do to see one of these foxes, was to go outside the cabin  about dusk when a shy but hungry fox dropped by for a handout.

As an outdoorsman, the primitive accommodations were easily endured because of the opportunity for exhilarating hikes and firsthand observations of offshore and island wildlife and vegetation. As a veterinarian on assignment, I hoped that the research I was doing and the samples taken would be helpful and, a few months later, a conclusion, brought about by previous research, my findings and that of those who followed me, was reached. The scientists who continued to study and probe the problem determined that the sea lion pups were dying because of environmental contaminants, PCBs and DDT compounds. At this time, due to environmental awareness and bans on certain products, the sea lions of San Miguel are again producing healthy pups.

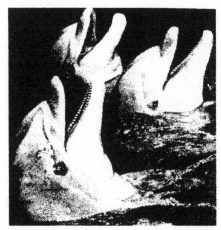

During one of my four trips to Hawaii to inspect the Atlantic bottlenosed dolphin area, examine them and exchange ideas with the veterinarian stationed there, I had the opportunity to observe a dolphin training exercise in the waters off Oahu. The day's outing was unforgettable and this animal remarkable.

The trainer, the skipper of the boat and I headed towards the training grounds. The boat looked like most twelve-foot open cockpit motor boats except for the two round signal spots about six inches in diameter painted on the port side of the boat near amidships. The forward spot indicated "yes," the aft one "no" and the trainer with a bucket of fish stood inside the boat between the two areas. Rex, the dolphin, followed along this marked side of the boat, about two feet away and at the surface. Suddenly, without the trainer signaling him, the dolphin streaked off. The skipper stopped the boat and I looked at the trainer quizzically.

"He's picked up something with his sonar. It could be something as far as a quarter of a mile away and he's too curious not to check it out."

In about ten minutes, Rex returned, bumped the side of boat with his nose to indicate he was ready to proceed and we sped forward, continuing on to the designated area.

"Doesn't he get a reward for returning?" I shouted over the drone of the engine.

"No, not this time because I did not signal him to leave. When he does a behavioral pattern on his own, he's not being bad, he won't get scolded, but he won't be rewarded either because he was not supposed to leave."

In less than fifteen minutes we arrived at the training area, ready to start the practice session. Yesterday, the trainer had placed various objects on the sandy ocean bottom at a depth of about twenty feet and today it would be the dolphin's job to find them.

At the trainer's orders, the skipper slowed the boat, then shifted to neutral. We rocked gently from side to side in the almost flat waters of the bay.

"The search areas I'll signal him to check out may or may not have objects for him to find. I think you'll be amazed at his quick and definite responses." The trainer lifted his hand, signaling the dolphin to begin his search.

Rex swam slowly in about a ten-foot diameter circle off the side of the boat. He returned and thumped the "no" mark on the boat, indicating he had found nothing and swam out about three feet from the boat. The trainer nodded and the skipper put the vessel in forward, heading on to the next area, then idling the engine when we reached the proper location. This time, before we were at the site area and before the trainer signaled to search, the dolphin made quick excited motions indicating that he had located something with his sonar.

The trainer gave the hand signal, the dolphin went around in about a three-foot diameter circle and hit the "yes" mark.

"Good, fella," the trainer said, beaming with pride over the adeptness of his dolphin who was making happy, verbal noises, obviously pleased with himself, too. He reached into the bucket, pulled out a fish and handed it the dolphin. "Are ya ready to do our next maneuver?" he asked, as if the mammal could understand.

Maybe it did, too, because the dolphin raised out of the water, swaying back and forth in a "yes" manner while making agreeable dolphin sounds. The trainer leaned over the gunnel and placed a nose cone on the dolphin.

"This next exercise is an extremely important and valuable one. The purpose of it is to have the dolphin find and mark the location of an object. Sometimes these are potentially dangerous ones such as a bomb or torpedo. Because of this, Rex has been taught not to touch the object but to push the nose cone into the sand a few feet away from it. As soon as the cone is off his nose, a buoy is automatically deployed and floats to the surface, marking the spot. Then a frogman or diver can go down and retrieve or disarm the object."

As soon as Rex got the go-ahead signal, he dived, disappeared and was back at the boat by the time the orange buoy appeared in the distance, bouncing on the water's surface. He opened his mouth awaiting his fish reward.

"Amazing!" I said, shaking my head in awe at the speed the task was accomplished and the intelligence of this amiable animal.

During the next two hours, Rex was put through his exercises about twelve more times with a one hundred percent correct score. The dolphin followed alongside while we headed back to the base. When we reached his pen, he entered it agreeably.

"He seems quite happy to be back," I commented.

"Of course. He knows that now he'll get many fish as a reward, not just one at a time."

14

Trekking Through Thailand

My one-year adventure to a part of the world I had never seen was about to begin. I was going to Thailand! I had learned the Thai language, about their culture and customs, been briefed on my duties and was anxious to get under way. I wanted to see the many and varied things I had learned and to experience firsthand those that, as yet, I knew nothing about.

It was 1968, during the Vietnam War, I was a major in the US Air Force veterinary corps heading overseas to supervise a variety of interesting civic action programs. I would be involved with livestock disease control for hoofed animals, rabies control programs for small animals, food supplies and water and sanitation for US and Thai civilians and troops.

I boarded a military 707 transport in Washington, DC bound for Bangkok, then switched to a military C-130, a smaller plane, to go up country to my home base, Nakhon Phanom Royal Thai Air Force Base, about seven miles from Nakhon Phanom, a town across the Mekong River from Laos. About forty flying hours later, I arrived.

I had little time to settle in because the next day, I was off on my first assignment to the remote town of Loey. I had been told to wear casual civilian clothes and that I would be traveling in an unmarked military jeep because it was better to keep a low profile than be highly conspicuous while traveling through the back country. The purpose of this overland trip was to check on an agricultural program and meet with the Thai veterinarian stationed at Loey.

Major William McKenzie, an Air Force veterinarian who I would soon replace, and I left early that morning and headed southwesterly towards the town of Khon Kaen where Bill told me we would spend the night. It seemed to me that we could go farther that day than the 200 miles to this town but Bill must have his reasons. I would just sit back and enjoy the scenery and the day.

I thought that all of Thailand would be jungle-like but this area was like a savanna with scraggly trees and brush interspersed with patches of cultivated land. The two-lane road was paved near the small villages we passed but otherwise it was a rough, dirt road with numerous potholes. We had no protection from the bright sun in the open jeep, and although it was hot and sticky, the forty miles an hour we averaged produced a most welcomed cooling breeze. We stopped occasionally to see points of interest and that, combined with the road conditions, put us in Khon Kaen late in the afternoon. I now knew why Bill planned to spend the night here!

Khon Kaen was a clean, well-manicured town with colorful flowers planted here and there and many trees providing shade. We stayed in a typical Thai motel that had individual cottages as opposed to the one-large-building motel style in the States.

The next morning, soon after leaving town, we went over a pass and dropped down into a valley formed by the mountain ranges on either side of us and headed north. Although road conditions had not changed, the vegetation was more jungle-like with denser undergrowth and taller trees. It took about four hours to drive the 150 miles to the isolated town of Loey, the provincial capital. Loey is south of the Mekong River and on the northeastern edge of a mountain range that runs north to south through the middle of Thailand and acts as a barrier to east-west travel or commerce. In other words, Loey and this veterinarian were out in the boondocks.

The Thais had an interesting way of deciding who gets assigned to what area of the country. It seems that if a person is talented, he probably remains in Bangkok, if he were not so good, he would be sent to the capital of a nearby, well-populated province, and if he were not even that good, he would be sent farther out. This native veterinarian could not possibly go any farther afield.

We soon discovered one of the reasons he was sent to this faraway place. He had been instructed to build pit silos, holes in the ground where forage for animals could be placed. If crops were tended properly, seven crops a year could be harvested so storage areas were important. He had followed his orders and built them, however, he had dug the holes at the lowest part of the area. Every time it rained, rainwater as well as cattle manure washed down the slope and into the silos.

Bill and I politely told him how he could correct this undesirable situation. After several more hours of discussing his problems and offering solutions, we needed to move on to our next stop, the Air Force base at Udon Thani, so declined his invitation to stay over night.

We planned to drive east, over a mountain pass arriving at the base about dusk. Unfortunately, we got a late start and although we made fairly good driving time on this paved two-lane road, by the time we neared the top of the pass, it was already dark. We had heard unconfirmed reports about insurgent activity in this locale caused by either the Communists, the anti-government nationalists or drug runners. We definitely were concerned about our safety and we had a right to be because just ahead, we saw lights.

Bill slowed the jeep and we inched forward, debating whether to turn around and head back or proceed. We stared ahead, trying to detect anything that might indicate if the silhouetted male figures were allies. By now, we could see that the lights were vehicle headlights and the men milling about had guns!

My mouth was as dry as a cotton ball and my heart pounded so fiercely I thought surely Bill could hear it. I looked at him just as he looked at me and we both shook our heads. Whoever those men were — friends or adversaries — they had seen us and we had no choice but to go ahead.

As we moved closer, we could see six or seven armed men at a makeshift wooden barricade placed across the road. One guard stepped forward and shouted in Thai, "Stop. Who are you? What are you doing here?"

We were wondering exactly the same thing about them because, like us, they wore civilian clothes. However, there was no doubt about the seriousness of this situation because all rifles were aimed at us.

"This is a Thai Army check point," he yelled.

Bill answered quickly, "We are American military officers. Here's my identification." He held his military ID card in his outstretched hand.

"Both of you. Step out of the jeep and show your papers," he commanded, motioning at us with his gun and walking closer.

We did as he ordered as fast as we could, holding our cards in front of us so he could read them with his flashlight. The guard scanned them, then our faces, then back to the identifications.

"It's okay," he yelled over his shoulder in Thai. "They're Americans!"

Phew! Bill and I breathed an enormous sigh and smiled at each other. Once they knew we were Americans, the guards were most friendly. We found out that they were not regular Thai army but militia, sometimes called ir-regulars, which explained why they did not wear uniforms. We chatted for a time and even though they wanted us to stay the night, we needed to push on. They removed the barricade and we sped off, waving and shouting farewells over our shoulders.

Our conversation during the next hour and a half going down the dark mountain road to Udorn centered around the day's activities but in particular, our encounter with the military.

"What a day!" I exclaimed. "Since I've only been here less than a week, I'm wondering, Bill, is life here always this exciting?"

The next day, Bill and I hopped in the jeep and drove for about four hours to another province where our assignment was to determine what kinds of programs were needed to help with livestock care. Major John Allen, an US Army veterinarian stationed in Bangkok, was already there discussing beef cattle, his project, with the local Thai veterinarian, Doctor Prasat, assigned to this province and the person we had come to assist.

Doctor Allen's assignment was to develop a strain of beef cattle that would produce more meat for the Thais than their native, scrawny cattle did. Simply bringing in and raising American beef cattle was not the solution because they cannot stand the heat and humidity and had to be kept in air-conditioned barns. But, Doctor Allen imported hardy Brahma bulls from Texas, crossbred them with the local cattle and developed a breed of cow whose offspring could handle the heat better, withstand insects and the tropical diseases that were endemic to Thailand such as pasteurellosis, also known as shipping fever, brucellosis, calf scours, foot rot and others. Doctor Allen thought this would be a good area for some of his sturdy cattle and asked Doctor Prasat if he would like to care for some of them.

The Thai veterinarian had no knowledge of this crossbreeding program nor, for that matter, much of anything happening outside of his town because veterinarians assigned to remote areas seldom got out of the village. In addition, they were never given much money nor the authority to instigate new programs. Generally, they ended up like this doctor, developing small animal clinics. Although Doctor Prasat said he would like to be a part of Doctor Allen's program, he did not have the permission nor the funds to do so.

In the States, it would be a simple matter for a veterinarian to contact his superiors and discuss a situation like this but here it was different. In the Thai chain of command, subordinates generally do not initiate discussions until contacted by their superiors. This makes it difficult, to say the least, for the local veterinarian to communicate with Bangkok officials unless Bangkok communicated first.

After discussing his dilemmas, we developed a few viable ideas. One in particular would be quite helpful: I would act as a spokesperson between Doctor Prasat and the officials at the Thai Department of Agriculture.

Driving the road back to Bangkok was almost as thrilling as the events of the night before. Like the English, they drive on the left-hand side of the road. Even though the road was two lanes, frequently there would be four types of vehicles passing abreast at one time: a truck, a taxi, a water buffalo pulling a cart and us. Vehicles were dodging in and out and often all were on the wrong side of the road. Car horns were blaring constantly because it is impossible for a Thai to drive without one hand on the horn. The noises and confusion reminded me of driving in Mexico.

About an hour before reaching Bangkok, we knew we would drive by a dairy farm managed by a veterinarian from Denmark. This was an important and productive dairy farm that sent processed milk all over the country and we had heard glowing reports about his program and results. Under his supervision, he and his staff had crossbred local cows with imported ones to improve milk production and were teaching selected Thai farmers how to raise and care for the cows. We decided it would be beneficial for us to stop to see his results, offer our assistance and exchange data on cattle.

This farmer training program, funded jointly by the Thai and Danish governments, had more benefits for the farmer than just learning how to care for the animal because, after the farmer had completed the program, he was given a pregnant cow <u>and</u> a piece of land. The land plot was small, approximately two hundred feet deep by seventy- to eighty-feet wide, yet it was big enough for a grazing pasture, a garden and a cottage. The program was successful because it created an ongoing source of income for the farmer. He could sell or trade his marketable products — the calf when it was old enough; the excess milk from the cow; and fresh vegetables and fruit from the garden. Because crops grow rapidly and the farmer had access to the Danish-managed breeding program, the cycle could soon begin anew.

Another reason this was such a successful program was that the Danish veterinarians assigned to Thailand were not given a time limit as US military personnel are but were told by their government, "Don't return until you've completed your job." These Danes had already been here ten years.

Once back in Bangkok, Bill and I checked into the US military officers' hotel, The Chao Phraya. That evening, Bill showed me around the city, and even though I have always been a good navigator who seldom gets lost, to this day, Bangkok is a city that is most confusing to me. The land is flat with no visible landmarks, such as mountains, to get a bearing from, many of the streets are built on filled-in canals that wind around and the name of the same street can change every two or three blocks.

The next day, Bill and I met with the heads of the Thai Departments of Public Health and Agriculture and their staffs. The atmosphere was cordial and I was assured of their cooperation and support for continuing Bill's programs as well as any that I might initiate.

As the all day meeting began to wind down and when they learned that Bill had only a few days remaining in their country, they insisted on honoring him with a going away dinner. We were whisked away to a nearby Chinese restaurant where they presented Bill with a farewell remembrance gift of an exquisite piece of native artwork.

The waiters began to place the many delicious smelling bowls and plates of food on the table and they were quickly picked up and passed around, each person helping himself as the food went by. But, as I glanced down at my only eating utensils, a pair of chopsticks, I knew I was going to have a problem. I had grown up in the Midwest where knives, forks and spoons are the way of life and because the art of eating with chopsticks was not a part of my pre-Thailand military curriculum, I was not quite sure how to use them.

All the Thais were staring at me, watching to see what I did. I suspected at the time but later knew for sure that they are pranksters at heart and, although in their culture they use tableware, not chopsticks, they thoroughly delight in testing a newcomer's ability with these elongated wooden toothpicks. I made their night, I am sure, with my awkward attempts to run down food. Finally, after the laughter died down, a waiter brought me a set of utensils that I knew how to use and I thoroughly enjoyed the excellent meal.

As time passed, I learned that Thai food was good with the exception that when a Thai said it was going to be hot or spicy, it was EXTREMELY hot and spicy. Hot and spicy Mexican was entirely different than the Thais' equivalent. I soon learned that I could order the hot sauce on the side and control the level of discomfort. Fish sauce, one of their mainstays, could be ordered with or without extra red hot peppers so once I discovered this, my meals became more tolerable.

A Thai delicacy that I ate and thought was tasty was a rice bird. These brown, sparrow-sized birds feed extensively on rice and, when cooked, tasted like squab. The plucked, cleaned bird was, I think, deep fat fried to a crispy consistency and eaten, meat and bones. It took three of these tiny birds to equal one small chicken breast.

Another unusual dish was the silk worm. The Thais put the worm, still in its cocoon, into a vat of boiling water and cook it until the silk threads can be removed. The threads were then wrapped around spindles and sent to cloth manufacturing plants. The cooked cocoon shell and worm remained and was served to me at the silk processing plant in the southeastern part of the country as finger food. I thought it tasted good, almost like unbuttered popcorn.

I tried almost everything offered to me except the Texas cockroach-sized beetle that also fed on rice. I guess what turned me off was the way it had to be eaten because it was like something out of a Star Trek episode. One had to pick up the live beetle, bite the head from the squirming body, spit it out, then eat the carcass. Ugh.

One official trip I made by myself was to inspect the establishments supplying food to the US Navy base at Sattaheep and Utapao Air Force Base, both located on the gulf of Thailand, south of Bangkok. The military purchased rations from local vendors whenever possible and, as far afield from doctoring animals as this job description sounds, one of a military veterinarian's duties is to inspect foods to make sure conditions are sanitary and foods are properly handled.

In this case, I needed to inspect a food supply company that I was told was on the border between two provinces. As it turned out, the province line went right through the middle of this plant! Now I had two provinces involved and the work became much more difficult. I had to negotiate not only the rules and regulations of our government but those of two other bureaucracies. It took about a week of meeting and negotiating with officials to finally satisfy all requirements.

I visited several of the sites where the crossbred beef cattle were pastured but one of these locations, Kanchana Buri, held a special interest for me for several reasons. The town of Kanchana Buri is west of Bangkok near the Burmese border and on a river near the rebuilt bridge made famous by the movie, *Bridge Over the River Kwai.* Close to town is a cemetery, well-maintained by the Thai government, with the graves of many allied soldiers who died while working on this bridge during World War

II. In this same area is a Thai cavalry base that had sixty or more of the most beautiful chestnut horses I have ever seen plus a well-trained veterinary staff to care for them.

Although making routine inspections were usually the job of the base veterinarian, in some cases they required my input as senior military veterinarian in the country. Frequently I enjoyed the pleasures of traveling to outlying radar sites in remote picturesque areas in the mountains that generally required an overnight trip. I inspected the food service areas and also examined and treated pets of US personnel, both military and civilian, stationed in these areas.

Americans are generally fond of animals and seem to collect pets wherever they live. The potpourri of pets I examined included dogs, cats, lizards, birds and chickens — virtually, any animal that could be kept reasonably well as a pet. Because houses and barracks in tropical areas are built on stilts to keep them drier and well-ventilated, the protected area under the buildings made ideal shelters for pets and, in the Thais' case, for keeping livestock.

Even I ended up with a pet, a fairly large monitor lizard I named Henry. I kept him under my quarters at Nakhon Phanom in an enclosed area I made for him. Henry, a relative of a Komodo dragon, was blackish with white bumps, about three and one-half feet long and weighed about thirty pounds. He was partially tame and, although I could not pick him up and cuddle him, I could pet and walk him on a leash. I kept him a month but with my hectic traveling schedule he was not getting enough attention, plus, the women who cleaned the barracks were afraid of him, even though he was kept under the building, and asked if I would find some place else for him. Although he was bigger than most pet lizards, finding a new home for him was not that difficult because Thais are great animal lovers.

Almost every native in Thailand had a pet — a dog, cat, monkey, lizard, chicken or a bird. Even many Thai commercial establishments had pets. One well-known hotel in Bangkok kept a pet rooster near the front door that crowed a greeting to guests. In the tavern across the street from the hotel, the owner had a hornbill, a bird about the size of a goose with a bill almost like a toucan but thicker and wider and not quite as long and with a most unusual topknot, called a casque, on its head.

Songbirds were most popular with the natives and were such a part of the family that, when the owners went to town on weekends, they took their birds in elaborate, hand-woven cages. The central part of the town where everyone gathered was filled with the enchanting songs of these birds.

Weekend markets, particularly in Bangkok, included a variety of smells, noises, activities and items for sale or trade. There were food and cold drink stands and so many birds, reptiles, puppies, kittens, tiny flying squirrels and other animals that it was like an enormous pet shop. For entertainment, near the market were kite-flying contests with expert handlers maneuvering their elegant kites.

Ubiquitous lizards were present even in houses and served the vital purpose of catching bugs and flying insects that abound in tropical climates and, for me, they provided entertainment. In my quarters, these six- to seven-inch long tan acrobats liked to congregate around the bare bulb hanging from the center of the ceiling and I delighted in watching them. One evening, I was trying to read and watch television when I became distracted by two of them chasing each other near the overhead light. They got into a territorial scuffle, lost their footing and crashed to the floor right in front of me. They got up, shook themselves and both scrambled back up the wall to the ceiling light bulb to begin their challenges anew.

W hile at my home base, I noticed that previous veterinarians had established a labeled snake collection in about twenty bottles and jars. I had brought an US Navy textbook on poisonous snakes of Southeast Asia from the States so one weekend, I decided to key these pickled specimens with my book to see if they were titled properly. With the help of my sergeant, we opened each jar, laid out the snake, counted the scales, looked at the shape of the nose, the ears, its overall size and so forth to determine the type of snake. I discovered that about one-third of the bottles were mislabeled. Not only was the name of the reptile incorrect but, some that were tagged nonpoisonous were poisonous and vice versa. Although time-consuming, we correctly relabeled the jar with the proper snake in it and put new formaldehyde in each container.

Because I found that some local snakes were not in the collection, I put the word out that if someone found a snake, let me know and I would come and get it. However, the Thai civilians and military were not fond of snakes and even when someone did call me, usually by the time I got there, the snake had been beaten to a pulp.

I was particularly anxious to get a Chinese cobra, a highly dangerous, venomous snake because our collection did not have one. I never did get one in good condition, only a nearly unrecognizable, pulverized corpse.

I really thought I was lucky when a Thai brought me two live snakes in a box. Unfortunately, I was just leaving for a meeting and I did not have time to do anything but put them in a sturdier container and go. Alas, the next morning when I looked at them, they were dead. One was a poisonous viper and the other was a constrictor and although they would have made interesting additions to my live collection, at least I could still use them in the pickled one. After that, I always separated snakes until I could identify them and then release, cage or properly preserve them.

Because of my interest in Southeast Asia regarding poisonous water or land snakes, rodents or any animal that could cause diseases to the troops, on my way back to Thailand from a side trip to Japan, I stopped in Taiwan at an US military research station. Among their collections was a live snake exhibit. One colorful snake in particular caught my eye, a Taiwan beauty snake. It was about four feet long and one inch in diameter with an upper body of olive yellow to yellow gray, tinged with varying shades of green and black and numerous irregularly shaped designs and longitudinal bands. I was familiar with handling snakes and knew this was one was nonpoisonous so I opened the cage, reached in, thought I was grabbing it right behind its head but instead, I caught it too far back. It twisted its head around and nailed me with its sharp bony ridge of teeth.

"Ouch," I cried out.

The two staff personnel rushed over quite concerned because they did not know which snake had bitten me and I was bleeding profusely. They cleaned and disinfected the wound that, lucky for me, was not serious. I again reached into the cage and this time correctly captured the snake. One of them took a picture of me holding the snake even though I did not need a souvenir photograph because I have a permanent memento — the scar on my right hand.

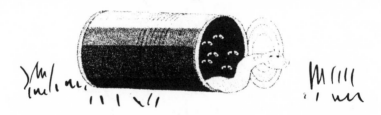

"Come quick!" the US Air Force medic shouted. "Doctor Arnell needs you. One of the Thais was bitten by something and the Doc thinks you might know what it was."

This was not an unusual request from a physician because I was known to have an excellent knowledge of the local fauna and also, by now, I was able to speak both the local and mountain Thai dialects and delighted in talking to the workers in their own dialect.

I dashed the short distance to the base dispensary where the frightened man was waiting. I looked at his bites that went from the top of his head right down his back to the waist of his pants. As I examined the wounds, I talked to him in Thai to find out where he had been and exactly what had happened. My conclusion was that a centipede had fallen from the tree he was working under and, as it bounced down his back, had bitten him at each place it landed. Although centipedes in Thailand are bigger, about six inches long and one to one and one-half inches wide, and more potent than the variety found in the States, the man would be all right.

Another of my assignments centered on a rabies vaccination program that was used throughout the country. And, when it came to a stray, or any dog for that matter, I took the position that all dogs were rabid until proven otherwise because rabies was present in all parts of Thailand. The Thais were familiar with the disease so I had no problems in getting their cooperation regarding vaccinations for their animals. The major problem was with the cost of the vaccine. Because it came from the US, and was expensive to import, ideally, the Thais should produce their own vaccine and they were trying.

The Thai laboratory near Bangkok had been attempting to manufacture one but, after I visited it I found they really needed the help of an expert in vaccine production. At my first convenient opportunity, I called the US Army veterinarian in Japan who was familiar with vaccine production techniques and I relayed the information he gave me to the Thais. This helped them to some extent however, by the time I left, they still had not produced a good vaccine.

Our vaccines, whether for dogs or hoofed stock, were given to teams composed of an US Air Force veterinary sergeant or technician and a Thai veterinarian and his technician who would go to villages and vaccinate animals. I traveled with them sometimes although most of my work consisted in coordinating programs and communicating with the Department of Public Health personnel in Bangkok, territory officials and country veterinarians or sanitarians, the Thai title for those who had limited veterinary education or experience.

On a trip I made with one of these teams, we loaded the jeep with supplies and left from Ubon heading towards remote villages to give rabies vaccinations to dogs. We bumped along the dirt trail, going deeper into woods, and it got hotter, more humid and miserable. The Thai veterinarian who saw the perspiration I was constantly wiping from my face asked if I was thirsty.

"Yes," I replied without hesitation, looking around for a refreshment stand but only seeing trees.

He stopped the jeep, took off his shoes, rolled up his pant legs and climbed a tree, machete in hand. "Watch out below," he yelled as he dropped four coconuts. He descended, whacked off the tops of the coconuts and we drank. How refreshing.

From there, we headed through the woods until we came to a clearing with three houses. I thought to myself, all this way just to inoculate the three or four dogs that must be here. What a wasted day.

As soon as we stopped, the Thai veterinarian switched on the jeep's loud speaker, turned up the volume and announced our presence. Within fifteen to twenty minutes, men, women, children and their one or more dogs appeared. At the end of two hours, we had vaccinated at least one hundred dogs!

I soon discovered that a large turnout like this was typical of a usual rabies vaccination day in the country: Although only a few houses, people or animals may be visible, there are many more unseen ones. This program was popular with the natives and, when I left, was still well attended and appreciated.

The following day, we went farther south, looking for the next village that wanted us to vaccinate their pets. It seemed we had traveled a long time and were unsure why we were not at the village yet. Finally, we saw houses in the distance. We got to the outskirts and saw a sign — a sign written in Cambodian! We estimated we had strayed about one mile into a volatile, unstable area. As inconspicuously and quietly as we could, we immediately did a one-eighty and headed back towards the safety of Thailand.

Without a doubt, while in Bangkok, I met one of the most influential men in my life, Doctor Boonsong Lekagul. He was the founder of the Association for the Conservation of Wildlife in Thailand and in the field of avians, he was Thailand's equivalent to Roger Tory Peterson, the famed American ornithologist. At that time, he was gathering information about the birds of Thailand and I became so engrossed with his project that as I trekked around the country, I took pictures of birds for him. It was the enthusiasm generated by him that, after I left the military, spurred me on to open a private practice specializing in birds. Doctor Boonsong published his book, *Bird Guide of Thailand,* supported by the World Wildlife Fund, and it is a wonderful, informative piece of literature. The book has intricately illustrated bird pictures, in-depth information on each bird and is a storehouse of avian information. Sadly, when I last returned to Thailand in 1986, he was so sick that he was unable to recognize me and I heard that he died shortly thereafter.

On one of my trips to the Royal Thai Air Force Base at Korat, I noticed the military police had a unique pet bird. It was the equivalent of a hawk yet its Thai name, *eo,* translated as eagle.

The next time I was there, I took along my camera to get a picture of it for me and Doctor Boonsong. I walked into the military police office and said in my best Thai, "I would like to take a picture of your *eo.*"

The officer nodded, looked a bit surprised but smiled warmly and said, "Of course. Follow me."

I walked behind him until he stopped in front of the latrine and pointed at the door.

What in the world! "No, no, your bird." This time I used the word *nouk* for bird.

"Ah," he said and led me back to a lounge area where the bird was caged.

The Thai language is tonal and has some words that are spelled the same but have different meanings depending upon the tone that is used. I had used the wrong tone which changed the word from meaning "eagle" to the word that means "to urinate!"

W hile at my home base, I managed the program for the Thai army's sentry dogs that included their physical exams and proper care. They had only eight dogs but caring for them was difficult because skin diseases prevailed due to the damp climate and parasitism flourished, particularly fleas. I found out that the veterinarian at Udorn had been using a new insecticide for these problems and it was working satisfactorily. I got some, read the label and discovered that the warnings were quite long and elaborate, especially regarding the hazards for the people administering it to the dogs. Because the animal had to be thoroughly bathed and lathered with the product while in the kennel bathtubs, it meant the insecticide would slosh all over anyone using it.

Naturally, I did not want either the Thai or US troops exposed any more than necessary to this product so I got rubber suits, boots and hats for them to wear while bathing the dogs. I explained to the men the dangers involved and why they should wear the protective gear, told them the proper procedures, the correct product concentration and the necessary time the product must be on the dog to be effective.

I left and returned about three hours later to find, much to my horror, that the men had taken off these outer garments because, "It's too damn hot!" There they were in their skivvies, in the tubs with the dogs, splashing the insecticide all over the place. I about had heart failure.

I immediately called one of physicians on the base. He dashed over, told all involved to decontaminate themselves by taking a shower and then to report to the dispensary immediately. He took blood from each man for testing that, fortunately, later showed there were no problems.

I patiently ran through the procedures again and told them why these rules must be followed. Because I could understand their discomfort in the hot rubber suits, we agreed that the bathing would be done at night when it was not quite as hot and humid. We also decided to try to find individuals to do the job who were more tolerant of the heat and humidity than others might be.

The weather in Thailand, in my opinion, is terrible. There are two seasons; wet and dry. I arrived there in June, about the middle of the wet season that starts about April and ends in September or October. During this time, it would rain so hard that if I put an arm out in front of me,

I could not see my hand. But the rains were localized; for example, it would rain for an hour and because the water could not run off fast enough, I would be standing in water up to my knees yet about a mile away, it would be desert dry. The canals this time of the year were all full, running with water and everybody was talking about the forth-coming dry season. I could hardly wait because as it was now, I was soaking wet all the time. I had to keep my billfold and any important papers in a plastic bag at all times. And, in addition to being humid, it was hot, in the ninety degree range, day in and day out. Yes, I thought, the dry season would be a pleasant change.

At last it quit raining but the natives neglected to tell me that the humidity never lessened. Now the weather was hot and humid without the benefit of a refreshing rain. Everyone and everything suffered. The rice paddies that had been knee-deep in water in the wet season were now so dry that the ground was scarred with gaping, ugly cracks. The humidity was high enough that I almost could wring water out of the air and a car passing by would kick up dust, the dust would settle down a bit and then fall to the ground as mud. By far, to me, the dry season was worse than the wet. It was truly miserable.

I counted the months and days until the rainy season returned and so did the Thais. They are so happy when it returns that they usher it in with a traditional water festival. This means, "Don't wear good clothes and always keep valuables in plastic because you will get wet." Everyone enters into the spirit of the celebration by throwing water balloons, shooting water pistols or running out of stores with a bucketful of water to toss on a passerby. Actually I thought it felt pretty good except for those few dousings by people who had discovered ice water.

A program concerned with the vaccination of water buffalo and some cattle for pasteurellosis was most interesting to me. This disease is a serious problem for the Thai livestock. Because it is a bacteria, not a virus, the preventive inoculation, properly called a bacterin instead of a vaccine, is relatively short lasting and the animal should have a booster injection every six months. Although giving these inoculations sounds rather routine and boring, it can be quite the opposite.

I went with my three-man team to a small village in the north central part of the country to inoculate water buffalo. The water buffalo is most important to the people: It is the tractor, pulling plows in the rice fields, dragging carts to and from the fields and providing an individual means of transportation. These docile, domesticated, large animals are a member of the bovine family, usually dark gray in color with fairly long, swept back horns and, because they are extremely nearsighted, they can be frightened easily.

We knew that the first problem in one of these mass inoculations was rounding up the buffalo so, we had notified the villagers ahead of time when we would be there and they had their thirty buffalo corralled in a specific area but not a fenced area. Undisturbed water buffalo will stay in a small herd at least for a while.

The next step was to restrain an individual animal. One common Thai method was, first, find as strong and as big a tree as possible. By our standards, even the big trees in this area were small, about eight inches in diameter by twenty feet high. About two feet out from the selected tree, they dug a two-foot-deep hole and placed a seven- to eight-foot-long post into it. Then, they tied a rope around one end of the post, moved the buffalo's neck against the trunk of the tree and wrapped the rope around the tree over the buffalo's neck and then around the post, which secured the buffalo's head to the tree. This clever, inexpensive holding device is similar to a stanchion used while milking cows.

The Thai veterinarian was helping me at the back of the first animal by holding the tail to get it out of the way while I cleaned the flank for the shot. The Thai technician was at the front of the animal, steadying the buffalo's head between the tree and post. The sergeant had prepared the syringe with the inoculation and had just handed it to me when — something spooked the buffalo!

It jerked its head up, lifting the entire tree and the post out of the ground. It stood for only a moment with the tree on one side of its head and the post on the other and then it headed out, lumbering about as fast as a scared cow. The Thai technician, holding on to the animal's horns for dear life, was trying to slow the animal down as he basically rode the horns of the buffalo backwards. The Thai veterinarian, hanging onto the tail, was almost flying. His feet barely touched the ground while he tried desperately to get the buffalo to slow or stop. The weight of the two slightly-built Asian men must have seemed about as heavy as two mosquitoes to the sturdy buffalo who did not appear to be the least bit bothered by their attempted halting efforts. In about one hundred feet, they reached the end of the clearing and disappeared into the woods.

I must have been an unusual sight, standing there with a surprised look on my face and the syringe in my hand ready to give the shot and no animal within pricking distance. The Thai villagers must have thought all of our behaviors were as exciting as a three-ring circus because they were shouting, applauding and laughing loudly.

Although it seemed a long time, it probably was only a few minutes when out of the trees came the buffalo, ridden by the veterinarian with the technician walking alongside. They smiled, waved as confidently as any conquering heroes and got an overwhelming ovation from their audience.

The tree and post were "missing in action" so we had to find another tree and dig another hole. Although buffalo are strong, probably a previous rain had thoroughly soaked the ground making it easier for the animal to uproot the tree. The second attempt to inoculate this buffalo — as well as the rest of the herd — was successful and uneventful when compared to this encounter.

We stayed for dinner in the village that night and the tale of the runaway buffalo was told over and over. The Thais love a good story and, doubtlessly, they are still telling this one.

Thailand was a wonderful place to have an overseas assignment. The people were friendly, happy, enjoyed humor and made me feel welcome. The food was good, the land beautiful in its own right and my adventures ranged from interesting to exciting. Although my tour of duty was one year, I had accrued some leave and decided to spend most of it there. Since then, I have been back to visit three times and plan to go again. The only thing I sincerely object to is — the weather.

Dean E. Ewing, DVM is a highly skilled veterinarian with a varied and remarkable career. He earned a BS and a DVM degree from Michigan State University and an MS from the University of Rochester Medical School. Dr. Ewing spent 22 years in the US Air Force with assignments in the space and Civil Defense programs, to Southeast Asia, and as the senior veterinarian for the US Navy marine mammals.

He has served as a board member for the San Diego County Veterinary Medical Association and the Association of Avian Veterinarians and as a delegate to the California Veterinary Medical Association. He also was elected as a Fellow of The Explorers Club. Dr. Ewing has authored numerous papers and is a renowned lecturer in the fields of avian, exotic and aquatic veterinary medicine. He is an inventor with two medical patents, developer of Bird Life, a pelleted avian diet, and founder of The Bird Center and Animal Hospital in San Diego.

Because of his achievements, he is included in *Men and Women of Science; 2000 Notable American Men;* and is listed in several biographical volumes including *Who's Who in Veterinary Science and Medicine;* and *Who's Who in North America.* He was awarded the US Air Force commendation and meritorious service medals.

He currently resides in Colorado and is a member of the Colorado Springs Area Veterinary Society, the American Veterinary Medical Association and the Association of Avian Veterinarians. With his more than 40 years of professional experience, Dr. Ewing continues to consult and, in this book, to share some of his experiences and advice to pet owners.

Shirley Herd graduated from the University of Kansas with a BS degree and has excelled as a versatile writer. She is a National Federation of Press Women award-winning columnist, has more than 500 magazine and news articles published and been a fiction and non-fiction book reviewer. She worked as a communication specialist, an advertising copywriter and a writer for TV and radio public service announcements. Because of her expertise, she is a frequent guest speaker or workshop director for private or professional organizations.

Herd is the author of four books: *The Cruising Cook; Easy Spanish; Blimey Limey! Wha'd He Say?*; and *Seawoman's Handbook*. She is listed in *Who's Who in the West; Writers, Editors and Poets; International Who's Who of Professional and Business Women*; and *International Writers and Authors*.

She lives in Colorado where she continues her writing career and, because of her love of animals, is a docent at the Cheyenne Mountain Zoo in Colorado Springs.